DEPARTMENT OF THE NAVY
HEADQUARTERS UNITED STATES MARINE CORPS
2 NAVY ANNEX
WASHINGTON, DC 20380-1775

I0415644

MCO P7010.20
MR
5 Aug 04

MARINE CORPS ORDER P7010.20

From: Commandant of the Marine Corps
To: Distribution List

Subj: MARINE CORPS COMMUNITY SERVICES NONAPPROPRIATED FUND PROCUREMENT POLICY
       (SHORT TITLE: MCCS NAF PROCUREMENT POLICY)

Ref: (a) SECNAVINST 7043.5B

Encl: (1) LOCATOR SHEET

1. Purpose. To publish policies for Marine Corps Community Services (MCCS) NAF
purchasing and contracting operations. This Manual offers guidance that MCCS
professionals can use to ensure the procurement operations run as smoothly as
the quality of life programs that procurement supports. The vision for the MCCS
procurement system is to satisfy the needs of the customer by delivering the
best value products and services to the MCCS on a timely basis, and in
accordance with applicable laws, regulations, and the reference.

2. Background. The former Marine Corps NAF procurement policy guidance was
issued prior to the creation of Marine Corps Community Services. Since then
there have been significant changes in procurement training and warrant
requirements, use of technology in procurement operations, and standardization
in contract format and content. This Order updates all applicable laws and
regulations.

3. Waivers. Waivers from the policies contained in this Manual must be
authorized in writing from CMC (MR). All policy waivers will be requested and
issued through Marine Corps channels.

4. Recommendation. Recommendations concerning the contents of this Order are
invited. Such recommendations will be forwarded to CMC (MR) via the chain of
command.

5. Reserve Applicability. This Manual is applicable to the Marine Corps Total
Force.

6. Certification. Reviewed and approved this date.

H. P. OSMAN
Deputy Commandant for
Manpower and Reserve Affairs

DISTRIBUTION: PCN 10209640600

     Copy to: 700
               0110(55)
               8145005 (2)
               7000144/8145001 (1)

LOCATOR SHEET

Subj: MCCS NAF PROCUREMENT POLICY

Location: _____
           (Indicate location(s) of copy(ies) of this Manual.)

MCCS NAF PROCUREMENT POLICY

RECORD OF CHANGES

Log completed change action as indicated.

Change Number	Date of Change	Date Entered	Signature of Person Incorporated Change

MCCS NAF PROCUREMENT POLICY

CONTENTS

CHAPTER

MCCS NAF PROCUREMENT POLICY

CHAPTER 1

PROCUREMENT AUTHORITY AND RESPONSIBILITY

CHAPTER 1

PROCUREMENT AUTHORITY AND RESPONSIBILITY

1000. PURPOSE

1. This Manual establishes policies and procedures governing procurements made with nonappropriated funds (NAF) within Marine Corps Community Services (MCCS). Other Marine Corps nonappropriated fund instrumentalities (NAFIs) are encouraged to adopt this policy guidance.

2. The goal of the NAF procurement system is to obtain products and services in a fair, equitable, and impartial manner, and to the best advantage of the MCCS. Accordingly, MCCS procurement personnel will:

    a. Conduct procurement actions with integrity and fairness;

    b. Perform in a timely, high quality, and cost-effective manner;

    c. Solicit team commitment and employ planning as an integral part of the overall process of acquiring products or services;

    d. Promote competition in the procurement process;

    e. Comply with applicable laws and regulations.

1001. EXCEPTIONS AND CLARIFICATIONS. Written requests for exceptions and clarifications will be sent through the chain of command to CMC(MR).

1002. DELEGATION OF PROCUREMENT AUTHORITY

1. CMC(MR) establishes MCCS NAF procurement policy and procedures, procurement training requirements, and appoints NAF contracting officers and purchasing agents via a warrant.

2. The Installation Commander (or the AC/S or Director, MCCS, if designated) has the responsibility to:

    a. Nominate contracting officers and purchasing agents;

    b. Ensure contracting officers and purchasing agents receive the required training;

    c. Exercise fiduciary responsibility by reviewing contracts and purchase orders, as desired.

3. In accordance with their warrant, NAF contracting officers and purchasing agents are delegated the authority to obligate MCCS, to the extent funds have been approved and made available by the requiring activity.

4. NAF procurement personnel may not obligate appropriated funds unless separately authorized under appropriated fund procurement regulations.

1003. APPOINTMENT AS CONTRACTING OFFICER OR PURCHASING AGENT

1. A warrant is the instrument by which CMC(MR) grants individuals the authority to enter the MCCS into legally binding contracts. This authority recognizes an employee's qualifications to be appointed as a NAF contracting officer or purchasing agent. Throughout this document, the title "Contracting Officer" and "Purchasing Agent" will be considered interchangeable as appropriate. Upon recommendation of the installation commander (or AC/S or Director, MCCS, if designated), assignment to a procurement position, and completion of applicable training requirements, the Director, MR Division will appoint the individual as contracting officer or purchasing agent granting the authority to execute and administer contracts on behalf of MCCS.

    a. The command nomination will specify whether the individual is to be appointed as contracting officer or purchasing agent, the dollar level of the appointment, and any limitations on contract types. Purchasing agents will primarily handle unilateral (one-party) purchase orders and delivery orders whereas contracting officers will generally handle more complex bilateral (two-party) contracts. Nominations will document the individual's experience, education, and training level, per paragraphs 1005 and 1006.

    b. Exceptions to the qualification requirements in paragraphs 1005 and 1006 may be requested for individuals who, due to their experience or circumstances, should be granted contracting officer or purchasing agent authority. Requests should include the individual's name, training, education, experience, and whether the individual presently holds a warrant. Exceptions must be authorized by CMC(MR).

    c. If the nominated employee does not meet requirements of paragraphs 1005 or 1006 and has not been authorized a waiver, CMC(MR) will issue an Interim Warrant granting the authority to execute and administer contracts on behalf of the MCCS for a specified period of time until the employee meets the specified training and education requirements.

2. Termination of appointment as a contracting officer or purchasing agent may be made for reasons such as unsatisfactory performance, reassignment, or termination of employment. Termination of procurement authority for unsatisfactory performance or reassignment will be made in writing by the installation commander (or AC/S or Director, MCCS, if designated). This notification must indicate the effective date of termination and may not be made retroactively. Termination of employment automatically terminates procurement authority. CMC(MR) will be notified of all terminations of NAF procurement authority.

1004. AUTHORITY OF CONTRACTING OFFICER AND PURCHASING AGENT

1. MCCS contracting officers and purchasing agents have authority to enter into, administer, or terminate contractual actions and to make related decisions. NAF contracts are contracts of the U.S. Government, but they do not obligate appropriated funds of the U.S. Contracting officers and purchasing agents may bind the MCCS only to the extent of the authority delegated to them. Contracting officers and purchasing agents will receive from the appointing authority clear instructions in writing regarding the limits of their authority. Information on the limits of authority will be readily available to the public and organizational personnel.

2. A contract action is defined as an award or modification of a purchase order, delivery order, or contract. Dollar value authority is applicable to each contract action. Contracting officers and purchasing agents will not amend or modify a contract that has a dollar value over the dollar limitations authorized by their warrant.

3. Guidance in deciding the dollar value in various contractual actions is provided below:

    a. Fixed dollar contracts - the amount of contract award, excluding option years;

    b. Indefinite delivery contracts, direct delivery agreements, open purchase orders, and blanket purchase orders - the value of the total estimated procurement for one year or lesser period (even if it is known that items and prices for later periods may be changed).

    c. Concession, vending and agency contracts - the estimated gross sales for the term of the contract.

    d. Contract modification - the value of the modification (not the value of the contract, as modified).

4. No contract will be entered into unless the contracting officer or purchasing agent ensures that all requirements of law, executive orders, regulations, and other applicable procedures, including clearances and approvals, have been met.

5. To meet the goals of MCCS, contracting officers and purchasing agents will be allowed wide latitude to exercise business judgment. Contracting officers and purchasing agents:

    a. Verify that the purchase request is complete, including all required signatures, certification of funds availability, and provides enough descriptive data to make the purchase.

    b. Be responsible for managing contractor relationships by overseeing the integrity and effectiveness of the procurement process, ensuring that contractors are treated fairly and objectively, and maintaining effective communications with contractors during contract performance.

    c. Take into consideration the advice of specialists in audit, law, finance, engineering, transportation, and other fields, as appropriate.

6. NAF contracting officers and purchasing agents will be guided by the Standards of Conduct as prescribed by Joint Ethics Regulation (DoD 5500.7-R) especially in the areas of conflicts of interest, favoritism, gifts and gratuities, and post Government employment. Questions will be directed to local Ethics Counselors.

7. DoD Non-Appropriated Fund civilian employees are subject to the same fiduciary responsibilities as appropriated fund civilian employees. Penalties for violations include administrative actions, monetary fines, or imprisonment (see 10 U.S. Code Section 147). Questions will be directed to MCCS Counsel.

1005. QUALIFICATIONS OF NAF CONTRACTING OFFICERS AND PURCHASING AGENTS

1. With the exception noted below, only U.S. Citizen Pay Banded (NF) and General Schedule (GS) salary plan civilian employees, or military personnel assigned to MCCS will be appointed as NAF contracting officers or purchasing agents. At the request of the AC/S or Director, MCCS, and upon the approval of MCCS Counsel, CMC(MR) may grant NAF contracting officer or purchasing agent authority up to $25,000 to local national employees in overseas locations. Legal aliens of the U.S. may be granted a NAF warrant with approval of the installation security officer. Such approval will be forwarded to CMC(MR) with warrant requests.

2. The designation of contracting officer or purchasing agent will be given to personnel currently engaged in the procurement function. Individuals who have been appointed as a contracting officer or purchasing agent as a collateral duty will retain their current job titles; however, when performing the procurement function they will do so as the contracting officer or purchasing agent.

3. In selecting contracting officers and purchasing agents, the nominating authority will consider the following, commensurate with the nominee's assigned responsibility:

    a. Demonstrated knowledge and experience in Government or commercial purchasing, contracting, contract negotiation, administration, or termination functions. This includes preparing solicitations, contracts, contract modifications, and supporting procurement documents; obtaining and analyzing product and price data for contract negotiations; and evaluating, reporting, and monitoring contractor performance;

    b. Demonstrated knowledge and experience in rental or lease of supplies, services, and equipment through open-market methods, placement of purchase orders, and placement of orders under blanket purchase agreements or indefinite delivery contracts such as Federal supply schedules, or other commercial purchase procedures;

    c. Demonstrated knowledge of the retail buying function, including review and evaluation of vendor products, price negotiation, placement of merchandise orders, product distribution, inventory control, and analysis of new trends;

    d. Demonstrated personal integrity and ability to apply sound business judgment.

1006. EDUCATION AND EXPERIENCE REQUIREMENTS FOR CONTRACTING OFFICERS AND PURCHASING AGENTS

1. The following education and experience benchmarks will be used in evaluating a nominee's qualifications for appointment as a contracting officer or purchasing agent:

    a. NF-3 or GS-5 through 8. Nominees should have one or more years of current (within last five years) contracting or purchasing experience with progressive assignments leading towards broader technical knowledge. The employee should have a high school diploma or equivalent;

b. NF-4 or GS-9 through 12. High school diploma or equivalent. Nominees should have two or more years of current, progressively complex and responsible procurement experience in MCCS, other Government agencies, commercial procurement, or retail buying. It is desirable that the nominee have completed at least two years of study at an accredited college or university leading towards a baccalaureate degree or have a two-year associates degree in a procurement-related field, such as business administration, accounting, or merchandising;

c. NF-5 or GS-13 and above. High school diploma or equivalent. Nominees should have three or more years of current, progressively complex and responsible procurement experience with MCCS, other Government agencies or commercial procurement. It is desirable that the nominee have a bachelor's degree from an accredited college or university that included or was supplemented by at least 24 semester hours in a field of study directly related to procurement, such as contracts, purchasing, contract law, accounting, business finance, merchandising, economics, marketing, or organization and management.

2. Procurement training is the cornerstone of professional development. To enhance professional capabilities of procurement personnel, training criteria for appointment as a contracting officer or purchasing agent is defined at paragraph 1007.

1007. TRAINING AND WARRANT LEVELS FOR NAF CONTRACTING OFFICERS AND PURCHASING AGENTS

1. MCCS contracting and purchasing personnel must satisfactorily complete procurement training as follows:

a. Warrant level - $10,000. To qualify for a warrant to purchase/contract up to $10,000, completion of the Army MWR or Navy MWR Basic Contracting or equivalent course is required;

b. Warrant level - $25,000. To qualify for a warrant to purchase/contract up to $25,000, completion of the Army MWR or Navy MWR Advanced NAF Contracting or equivalent course is required;

c. Warrant level - $100,000. To qualify for a warrant to purchase/contract up to $100,000, completion of the training required for the $25,000 warrant and the following contracting courses are required:

(1) Contract Formation or Source Selection;

(2) Contract Negotiation Techniques;

(3) Contract Price Analysis;

(4) Contract Administration;

(5) Contract Law.

These courses may be obtained from APF and/or NAF sources, as well as commercial firms who develop courses to meet Federal Government training requirements. Each course will provide 40 hours procurement training.

    d. Warrant Level - $300,000. To qualify for a warrant to purchase/contract up to $300,000, completion of the training required for the $100,000 warrant and the Army and Air Force Exchange Service Concession Contracting course or a 40-hour Performance-Based Service Contracting course is required.

    e. Warrant Level - $1,000,000; $10,000,000; or Unlimited. Based on the size of the command and dollar volume of the support service or revenue generating contracts awarded, the contracting officer must complete the contracting training above in paragraph 1007.1c and d., and one of the following;

        (1) Have a certification or associates degree in the procurement field, or;

        (2) Have at least 24 semester credit hours or equivalent in contracts, purchasing, contract law, accounting, business finance, merchandising, economics, marketing, or organization and management, or;

        (3) Have an undergraduate degree from an accredited college or university, or;

        (4) Have at least 10 years of experience in the procurement field.

    f. Construction Warrant. Individuals seeking a NAF construction contracting warrant must complete the contracting training above in paragraph 1007.1c and d., as well as the training specified by the Naval Facilities Engineering Command (NAVFAC). Contact CMC (MR) for additional guidance.

2. Course or education equivalency will be determined by CMC(MR). Individuals holding a Certificate of Appointment as an MCCS contracting officer or purchasing agent as of 1 January 1999 are grand fathered from mandatory attendance at core courses. Contracting and purchasing personnel with a warrant of $25,000 or greater will receive a minimum of 40 hours annual procurement training.

3. Appropriated fund GS-1102 and 1105 personnel assigned to NAF procurement positions will comply with appropriated fund acquisition training, education, and experience requirements. Attendance at NAF procurement training courses is not required if the equivalent appropriated fund training courses have been completed.

1008. CONTRACT REVIEW AND APPROVAL. The request for a warrant may include the dollar volume at which a higher-level review and approval will occur (i.e. the purchasing agent may have a $100,000 warrant; however, his or her supervisor may elect to review all purchases over $25,000 prior to award). The purchasing agent will sign the order, but the reviewing official will document his review and approval on a separate document prior to award. This documentation will be retained in the contract file. Supervisors will not apply undue influence to coerce contracting officers or purchasing officials to perform unlawful or ill-advised procurements.

1009. LEGAL SUPPORT AND REVIEWS. The Office of Counsel for the Commandant (CL), and its field offices are component offices of the Navy Office of General Counsel and will provide legal support and assistance to MCCS and NAF contracting activities worldwide. All NAF procurement personnel are strongly encouraged to submit all questions of a legal, policy, or business nature on any subject that is of concern to them to their regional MCCS Counsel. If no regional MCCS Counsel is available, inquiries should be made to CMC(MR). Each request for legal review and assistance should include a statement of the issue, supporting documentation (including solicitation documents, contract files, etc), and any other information needed to assist in resolving the matter.

1. MCCS procurement personnel will obtain legal review, or consultation as appropriate, for the following:

a. All nonrevenue generating support service solicitations or contracts (including purchase orders and Blanket Purchase Agreements) anticipated to be in excess of $100,000;

b. All revenue generating patron service solicitations or contracts are anticipated to generate sales in excess of $300,000 over the term of the contract;

c. Solicitations or contracts recommending use of Alternative Dispute Resolution (ADR) procedures;

d. Determination of whether a proposed solicitation or contract supports the Exchange or MWR, and which Disputes Clause should be used when not clearly defined (Refer to paragraph 7108);

e. Proposed awards that may result in a contract period in excess of five years;

f. Proposed awards that may result from an unsolicited proposal;

g. Proposed awards that require the MCCS to sign the contractor's form, such as a license or support agreement;

h. Offeror mistakes alleged before or discovered after contract award;

i. All decisions concerning procurement protests (prior to and after contract award), inexcusable delays, claims, disputes, and appeals;

j. Cure notices, show-cause and forbearance letters, and supporting documentation;

k. Termination actions and supporting documentation;

l. Determination of whether a proposed service is for personal or nonpersonal services, when not clearly defined;

m. Entertainment contracts to which the Service Contract Act applies, a royalty and copyright clearance is required, or the nature of the entertainment may present a physical risk to the entertainers, the audience, or property;

n. All proposed contractual documents involving the purchase or lease of real estate or license to use real estate;

o. Substantive changes to approved contract formats;

p. Matters involving tax issues and MCCS tax status;

q.   Ratification of unauthorized commitments over $5,000 (see paragraph 1014);

r.   Recommendations for suspension or debarment of any MCCS contractor;

s.   All Congressional inquiries pertaining to MCCS contracting actions;

t.   Freedom of Information Act (FOIA) responses and questionable or controversial FOIA issues; and

u.   Questions regarding applicability and implementation of Federal statutes such as the Service Contract Act, Davis Bacon Act, etc.

2. Notice of Legal Sufficiency. Legal counsel will inform the contracting officer in writing whether a proposed action is legally sufficient (or the details of any insufficiency) and a recommended course of action to overcome the insufficiency. The contracting officer will take steps to overcome legal objections to the proposed action and document decisions reached. Documentation of legal review will be retained in the contract file.

1010. SEPARATION OF FUNCTIONS

1. The integrity of the procurement process requires that several distinct functions to be performed sequentially by different personnel. These are:

a.   The preparation of the purchase request and certification of funding availability;

b.   Approval of the procurement action (if required based upon the dollar volume of the action);

c.   The procurement action;

d.   Receipt of goods or services;

e.   Payment.

2. Small activities may not be able to assign separate personnel for each function; however, these duties must be separated to the maximum extent practicable to preserve checks and balances needed to preclude fraud, waste, and abuse. In no event will all of the above functions be performed by the same individual. Procurement personnel will not engage in receiving and/or invoice payment functions, or report to personnel responsible for those functions.

3. A limited exception to the separation of functions requirement is granted to individuals making purchases with a purchase card and individuals entering requisition and orders into an electronic purchasing system.

1011. PROCUREMENT INTEGRITY

1. By awarding a contract (including delivery or purchase orders) the contracting officer certifies that during the procurement process:

a. He/she will not directly or indirectly discuss, solicit or accept future employment or any business opportunity with the contractor or any offeror;

b. He/she will not ask for, receive or accept an offer, promise or gift of any gratuity, entertainment, money or other thing of value from an offeror or contractor;

c. No information proprietary to another offeror or other procurement information (listing of offerors, prices offered, technical evaluations or rankings, and so forth) will be disclosed or given to any person not authorized by the contracting officer, until it would be available to the public under MCCS procedures.

2. If the contracting officer cannot certify compliance with these restrictions, the award will not be made (or delivery order or purchase order issued) and the contracting officer will report the circumstances in writing to MCCS Counsel.

3. The Contracting Officer will inform all MCCS personnel involved with the procurement (i.e., requisitioner, technical personnel, evaluators, etc.) of these procurement integrity requirements.

1012. <u>PROCUREMENT SUPPORT</u>. In addition to the assigned responsibilities, MCCS procurement offices may support other MCCS activities or other NAF activities outside MCCS organizational responsibility. If support of other activities is to be handled on a continuing basis, a written Memorandum of Understanding (MOU) between the activities is recommended.

1013. <u>RATIFICATION OF UNAUTHORIZED PROCUREMENT ACTIONS</u>

1. An unauthorized procurement action is an agreement (either verbal or written) that commits MCCS funds and or resources to a concern that is not binding solely because the MCCS representative who made it lacked the authority to enter into that agreement on behalf of the Government. The ratification of an unauthorized procurement action is an after-the-fact approval of the purchase. An unauthorized procurement action purportedly on behalf of the MCCS may result in a void or void able contract and, in some circumstances, may result in the personal liability of the individual making the unauthorized commitment.

2. Unauthorized procurement actions up to $5,000 may be ratified by the senior contracting officer at the MCCS activity.

3. Unauthorized procurement actions that exceed $5,000 may only be ratified by the Installation Commander, unless this authority has been delegated to the AC/S or Director, MCCS. The AC/S or Director, MCCS, may in turn delegate this ratification authority to the senior MCCS contracting officer.

4. Unauthorized procurement actions exceeding $5,000 will receive legal review and approval prior to ratification.

5. To ratify unauthorized commitments, the supervisor of the individual who made the unauthorized commitment will prepare a request for ratification. The request will be sent to the ratifying official through appropriate channels as early as possible. The request will include the following information and documentation as appropriate to the circumstances:

a. Name of the individual who made the unauthorized commitment;

b. Date of the commitment;

c. Name and address of the company or individual to whom the commitment was made;

d. Item or service involved;

e. A copy of the vendor's invoice (including quantities with unit and total dollar amount);

f. The purchase request with supporting documentation;

g. A written, signed statement by the individual who made the unauthorized commitment explaining the circumstances of the commitment;

h. A statement of disciplinary action taken, or an explanation why none was considered necessary, and action taken to prevent recurrence of the unauthorized act;

i. Any other information or recommendation about the commitment and the individual making the commitment;

j. Recommendations regarding approval or disapproval, and the basis for making them.

6. Based on a review of the documents submitted, and concurrence by MCCS Counsel, the ratifying official will either ratify the unauthorized commitment, or prescribe an alternative course of action. If the ratifying official approves the purchase action, the contracting officer or purchasing agent will execute the appropriate purchase document.

1014. RELEASE OF ADVANCE PROCUREMENT INFORMATION. MCCS personnel will not provide potential contractors with advance information concerning proposed acquisitions. Such information will be released only by duly appointed contracting officers, acting within the scope of their authority.

1015. STANDARDS OF CONDUCT. The Joint Ethics Regulation (JER), and DoD Directive 5500.7 (Standards of Conduct) apply to all DoD components, including NAFIs.

1. Designated Ethics Counselors. Supervision of the Marine Corps ethics program is shared between the Staff Judge Advocate to the Commandant (CMC (JA)) and Counsel for the Commandant (CMC (CL)), who are the designated agency ethics officials (DAEOs) for the Marine Corps [MCO P5800.16A]. CMC (JA) and CMC (CL) provide ethics advice and training, and monitor financial disclosure reporting in their areas of responsibility. Staff judge advocates and local CL attorneys serve as ethics counselors and supervise the ethics programs within their commands or areas of responsibility.

2. Ethics Training And Financial Disclosure

    a. Those in contracting and procurement positions are required to have annual ethics training and to file annual Confidential Financial Disclosure Reports (OGE Form 450) with their designated Ethics Counselor. The purpose of filing is to identify possible conflicts of interest.

    b. Purchase cardholders purchasing less than $100,000 annually are not required to file OGE Form 450; however, all approving officials must do so.

    c. Individual supervisors may require additional personnel to have annual ethics training and complete OGE Form 450 if, in the supervisor's judgment, this individual is in a position to influence the integrity of the procurement process.

3. Gifts and Personal Purchases. MCCS personnel involved in procurement and related functions will not accept or solicit gifts given to them in their official capacity from any offeror or contractor, nor will they use their positions or influence to arrange for the direct purchase from any MCCS supplier of items for their personal use, or use by their families, or other MCCS employees. MCCS personnel will report the name, address, and circumstances of any request for personal preferential purchasing to the designated Ethics Counselor.

1016. REPORTING VIOLATIONS OF STANDARDS OF CONDUCT RELATING TO PROCUREMENT. Knowing and willful failure of MCCS personnel to report criminal conduct and standard of conduct violation to the MCCS supervisor may be grounds for disciplinary action. The contracting officer will obtain guidance from MCCS Counsel as to appropriate action when a procurement action is affected.

1017. POST EMPLOYMENT RESTRICTIONS. Current and former DoD employees may obtain counseling and written advice concerning post employment restrictions from the Ethics Counselor of the DoD command or organization from which they are leaving or have left federal Government service. Questions from MCCS procurement personnel should be referred to MCCS Counsel. The Joint Ethics Regulation, DoD Directive 5500.7-R, discusses the issue in detail as well as statutory restrictions applicable to former military and civilian personnel.

1018. PROCUREMENT REFERENCE LIBRARY. Each NAF procurement office will maintain a current file of, or electronic access to, applicable regulations, directives, local implementing instructions and other publications as needed for accomplishing the procurement function.

1. Standards of Conduct as prescribed by Joint Ethics Regulation (DoDD 5500.7-R). Internet address: www.dtic.mil/whs/directives.

2. SECNAV Instruction 7043.5B, Subj: Nonappropriated Fund (NAF) Procurement Policy, dated 18 Apr 02. Internet address: http://neds.nebt.daps.mil.

3. MCO P1700.27A, Subj: Marine Corps Community Services Policy Manual, dated 08 Nov 99, subsequent CMC(MR) policy letters, and regulations cited as references thereto.

4. Lists of Parties Excluded from Federal Procurement and Nonprocurement Programs. Internet address: http://epls.arnet.gov/.

5. U.S. Department of Justice UNICOR Federal Prison Industries Catalog. Internet address: www.unicor.gov.

6. National Industries for the Blind Catalog. Internet address: www.nib.org.

7. Department of the Treasury's Listing of Approved Sureties (Circular 570) for construction Performance and Payment Bonds. Internet address: www.fms.treas.gov/.

MCCS NAF PROCUREMENT POLICY

CHAPTER 2

ADMINISTRATIVE POLICY AND TAXES

CHAPTER 2

ADMINISTRATIVE POLICY AND TAXES

2000. UNIFORM PROCUREMENT INSTRUMENT IDENTIFICATION NUMBERING SYSTEM (PIIN)

1. MCCS solicitations and contracts (including purchase orders, delivery orders, and agreements) will be numbered in the format shown below. The basic contract number assigned to the document will remain unchanged for the period of the contract, including any extensions. The PIIN has been designed to allow report sorting by command, MCCS NAFI, fiscal year, and contract type. Sample MCCS Contract Number QUM04-C-0001 is described below:

COMPANY CODE & FY	CONTRACT TYPE	SEQUENTIAL NUMBER
3 character & 2 character	1 character	4 character

POSITION	CONTENTS	DESCRIPTION
1-3	Company Code	Three character company code
4-5	Fiscal Year	The last two digits of the fiscal year in which the document was prepared
6	Contract Type Code	One-character contract type code (see contract type code listing below)
7-10	Sequential Number	Four digit sequential number – begins with 0001 each fiscal year for each contract type

CONTRACT TYPE* CODES:
A   AGREEMENT
B   BLANKET PURCHASE AGREEMENT
C   CONTRACT
D   INDEFINITE DELIVERY CONTRACT (DEFINITE QUANTITY or INDEFINITE QUANTITY) (includes requirements contracts)
E   CONSTRUCTION CONTRACT
F   DELIVERY ORDER (placed against existing MCCS contracts or contracts of other Government departments/agencies)
G   BASIC ORDERING AGREEMENT
H   REVENUE GENERATING CONTRACT (concession, vending, pay telephones, etc.)
I   (Reserved)
J   (Reserved)
K   SHORT TERM COMMODITY CONTRACTS
L   INDIVIDUAL SERVICE CONTRACT (instructors, entertainers)
M   (See P)
O   BLANKET PURCHASE ORDER RELEASE
P   PURCHASE ORDER (use M when P exhausted)
Q   REQUEST FOR QUOTATION
R   REQUEST FOR PROPOSAL
S   RESALE PURCHASES (if made using the non-Exchange purchasing system)

T   (Reserved)
V   GOVERNMENT COMMERCIAL PURCHASE CARD PURCHASES
W   WAREHOUSE INVENTORY ITEM (Camp Butler only)
X   OPEN PURCHASE ORDER/BLANKET PURCHASE ORDER (formerly DIRECT DELIVERY CONTRACT)
Y   RECEIVER
Z   PURCHASE REQUEST

* See Chapter Six (6) for contract definitions

2. Merchandise purchased for Exchange resale are not required to follow this numbering system.

2001. CONTRACT FORMS PROVIDED BY THE CONTRACTOR. Signing contractor-provided contract forms on behalf of the MCCS is not authorized, unless prior concurrence has been obtained by MCCS Counsel.

2002. CONTRACT PERIOD

1. Generally MCCS contracts may be for any length of time up to five years. When contract requirements are repetitive, multi-year contracting is recommended. If future requirements are unknown, the contract may specify an initial contract period of one or two years, with contract renewal options up to a maximum of five years.

2. Revenue generating service contracts may be negotiated for longer than five years if contractor capital investment is required. See paragraph 5325 on Contractor Capital Investment and paragraph 5326 on Public-Private Ventures.

3. MCCS activities may negotiate support service contract periods exceeding five years under special circumstances, such as noncompetitive service agreements (i.e., utility services). CMC(MR) may negotiate multi-year system wide contracts for credit card processing, employee health insurance, etc.

4. MCCS Counsel will review and approve documentation supporting all contract periods greater than five years prior to contract award. This documentation will be retained in the official contract file.

2003. EXECUTION OF CONTRACT ACTIONS

1. Only contracting officers and purchasing agents will sign and execute NAF contract actions on behalf of the MCCS. The contracting officer/purchasing agent will personally sign all contracts, purchase orders, and supporting documents that require the signature of the contracting officer or purchasing agent.

2. The contracting officer or purchasing agent will ensure that the individual signing the contract for the contractor has authority to bind the contractor.

3. Order of Signatures:

    a. Unilateral instruments will be signed by the contracting officer or purchasing agent before sending to the contractor;

b. Bilateral instruments will be signed by the contracting officer or purchasing agent after they have been signed by the contractor, unless justified otherwise by the contracting officer or purchasing agent.

2004. <u>DISTRIBUTION OF CONTRACT INSTRUMENTS</u>

1. Contracting officers and purchasing agents will distribute copies of unilateral contract documents as follows:

    a. One copy to contractor with original signature;

    b. One copy to be retained in the procurement office (with original signature if available);

    c. One copy to the requesting activity or Contracting Officer's Representative (COR);

    d. One copy to the receiving activity if other than the requesting activity;

    e. One copy to the accounting office.

2. Bilateral contract documents will be distributed as stated above in paragraph 2004.1a and b; however, the contractor and the MCCS will both maintain original copies of the contract with original signatures. If the contract is lengthy, copies distributed to accounting and receiving may be limited to the signature page, list of items or services to be provided, price, and delivery or receipt and acceptance data.

3. Electronic copies may be distributed as above. Electronic signatures are authorized when using an electronic procurement system.

4. Additional distribution of contract documents should be only as required and kept to the minimum.

2005. <u>OFFICIAL PURCHASE FILE</u>

1. The purchase file will include the following for each action:

    a. Purchase request including specifications or statement of work with necessary approvals and certified funding data;

    b. Request for Quotes and price quotes received, or justification for noncompetitive procurement (see paragraph 6006);

    c. Completed Record of Negotiations form (401-R) or Justification for Award memorandum (see paragraph 6003.2);

    d. Purchase Order;

    e. Receiving Report (if available);

    f. Any other documents pertinent to the purchase.

2. Electronic documentation is authorized.

2006. OFFICIAL CONTRACT FILE

1. A contract file folder will be established and maintained by the contracting office for each contract action. The complexity of the purchase normally dictates whether a hard cover multi-tab contract file folder or a plain manila folder will be used. Generally, lengthy contracts for supplies, equipment, patron services and support services will be filed in multi-tab folders. Data will be filed in chronological order. The front of the multi-tab folder will be labeled with the PIIN. Regardless of the folder used, the contract file will contain the following data as applicable:

　　　a. Contracting Authority. Approved document requesting the contracting officer to proceed with the purchase action; for example, a purchase request with necessary approvals and certified funding;

　　　b. The statement of work, specifications, or purchase description forwarded by the requestor;

　　　c. Solicitation documents, including the Department of Labor Wage Determination for service contracts (see paragraph 5303), and any solicitation amendments or correspondence with potential offerors;

　　　d. Source list to which the solicitation was issued;

　　　e. Requests for review and approval, and review comments pertaining to the solicitation, award, and resulting contract;

　　　f. Proposal Register, identifying the firms who submitted a proposal, and the date and time of receipt;

　　　g. Summary or abstract of proposals, which lists the prices or fees proposed by each offeror;

　　　h. Evaluation documentation, which reviews and ranks the proposals submitted by each offeror;

　　　i. The envelope and any other relevant paperwork, which documents receipt of a late proposal (received after the date for receipt of proposals but prior to award);

　　　j. Any other documents pertinent to negotiation and award of the contract, including memorandums of telephone calls made and received;

　　　k. Justification for Award memorandum;

　　　l. Notice of Award Letter;

　　　m. Unsuccessful proposals;

　　　n. Notices to unsuccessful offerors regarding award;

　　　o. The contract document as awarded;

　　　p. Contractor performance or review documents, including inspection and audit reports;

q. Correspondence or memorandums of phone calls with the Contracting Officer's Representative (COR);

r. Contract administration documentation, including contract modifications (renewals or extensions), with appropriate justification for contract actions, and a record of any negotiations conducted, and updates to any Department of Labor Wage Determination;

s. Copies of all correspondence with the contractor;

t. Contract closeout records at the end of the contract period.

2. After awarding a contract, the contracting officer will review the contract file to make sure all required data is included. Original documents will be maintained in the official file. To avoid a cluttered file, duplicate copies and work papers not relevant to the solicitation or contract should not be in the file. All solicitation and contract actions (such as offer and award documents, contract modifications, memorandums, etc.) must be dated and signed.

2007. ADVANCE PAYMENTS. Advance payments may be provided on any type of contract. However, the contracting officer or purchasing agent will authorize advance payments sparingly. Advance payment is the least preferred method of contract financing and will not be authorized if other standard payments (partial, progress, and payment on receipt) procedures are available. If the terms of the sale require advance payment, the contracting officer or purchasing agent will coordinate with the MCCS accounting office to obtain a check to mail to the contractor.

2008. FIXED ASSETS. Fixed Assets (FA) is defined as NAF property and equipment with an expected life of two or more years, and costing $1,000 or more. FA may only be purchased by a contracting officer or purchasing agent. Requesting activities will identify if the item to be purchased is a FA on the requisition. When FA are ordered, the contracting officer or purchasing agent will provide the MCCS accounting office with a copy of the purchase document for recording and tracking purposes.

2009. RETIRING OFFICIAL PURCHASE FILES AND CONTRACT FILES

1. When a contract instrument (including purchase orders, delivery orders, and agreements) expires through termination or otherwise, the file will be retired under procedures set out in SECNAVINST 5212.5, Navy and Marine Corps Records Disposition Manual. Identify orders/contracts by number on the outside of each box and keep a list of the files in each box. Keep a master list of all boxes and files, with location of the boxes, in the procurement office so they can be retrieved should the need arise.

2. If a claim or dispute is ongoing or anticipated, the contract file will not be retired until the claim or dispute is settled.

2010. ANNUAL PROCUREMENT FORUM. The AC/S or Director, MCCS, will ensure that local meetings of NAF contracting and purchasing personnel, key operating personnel, and legal counsel are held annually to discuss improving procurement procedures. Representatives from the installation appropriated fund procurement office may be invited. Topics for discussion may include: sources of supply, comparison of prices paid for the same or similar items, and the consolidated procurement of common items. Where feasible, joint meetings for personnel from installations located in the same geographic area will be held.

2011. <u>TECHNICAL AND AUDIT ASSISTANCE</u>

1. CMC(MR) will periodically conduct technical reviews and management assistance visits of contracting and purchasing activities. Reviews will be documented with written reports that reflect significant observations, recommendations and areas of commendable performance or of serious deficiencies.

2. Reviews may be requested by the Installation Commander, AC/S or Director, MCCS.

3. Procurement personnel will respond to audit inquiries from internal auditors and commercial firms contracted to perform audit services.

2012. <u>GENERAL TAX RULES FOR NAFI'S</u>. As an instrumentality of the United States, an MCCS NAFI is entitled to the same immunity accorded the U.S. Government from the taxes of states, the District of Columbia, Puerto Rico, and territories and possessions of the United States. Contracting officers and purchasing agents will familiarize themselves with the applicability of taxes to purchases made and contracts awarded in their locality. When a tax question arises, contracting officers and purchasing agents will request assistance from MCCS Counsel.

2013. <u>STATE AND LOCAL TAXES IN THE UNITED STATES</u>. Contracting officers and purchasing agents will analyze each purchase action to ensure that MCCS does not pay inapplicable taxes.

1. The following types of purchases often have state and local tax implications that must be considered:

   a. Resale Merchandise - MCCS is not subject to direct state and local taxes on items purchased for resale;

   b. Beer and Tobacco Products - State and local excise taxes on beer and tobacco products are usually the responsibility of the distributor. The distributor's tax expense would normally be an element in determining its price charged to MCCS for the goods. Most states have provided some type of exemption from cigarette taxes on sales made to Exchange retail and Club operations; most states have provided some type of exemption or credit on sale of beer to Exchange retail and Club operations;

   c. Leased or Rented Equipment - Certain state and local taxes are the responsibility of the seller or lessor. Under these circumstances, assuming there is no independent exemption available on sales to the federal government, the vendor or lessor may include the cost of such taxes in the price charged to MCCS for the goods or services. The applicable law varies by state.

   d. Gasoline - MCCS is responsible for payment of federal, state and local

excise taxes on the sale of gasoline in the United States. Gasoline used in MCCS
or other Government vehicles may be exempt, depending on state law.

2. Refer any questions on taxes to MCCS Counsel.

2014. MANUFACTURER'S EXCISE TAX. Items purchased for overseas MCCS activities,
other than activities in Alaska and Hawaii, are exempt from the Federal
Manufacturer's Excise Tax by virtue of exportation.

2015. FOREIGN TAXES. MCCS is precluded from paying or collecting foreign taxes.
By virtue of international agreements, MCCS is exempt from most foreign customs,
duties and taxes. Specific advice must be obtained from MCCS Counsel.

2016. CONTRACTOR TAXES

1. MCCS contractors are responsible for payment of all federal, state, host
country, and local taxes applicable to the property, income, and transactions of
the contractor. When required by applicable laws and regulations, patron service
contractors will collect and remit sales taxes to the state.

2. To ensure compliance with federal tax requirements, each contract will include
the Taxpayer Identification Number (TIN), Employer Identification Number (EIN), or
Social Security Number (SSN) of each corporation or individual providing supplies
or services to the MCCS. This information will be forwarded to the MCCS accounting
office upon contract award.

CHAPTER 3

PROCUREMENT PLANNING

CHAPTER 3

PROCUREMENT PLANNING

3000. <u>GENERAL</u>

1. Procurement planning is the key to successful development of a requirement and subsequent execution of the procurement. Based on the complexity of the requirement, procurement plan participants will include representatives from contracting, fiscal, legal, technical and activity management areas. Contracting personnel will be involved in all phases of the procurement process, including procurement planning.

2. As part of the procurement planning process, MCCS program managers will research the market as a means of getting information on sources of supply and current state-of-the-art products and services. Suppliers/vendors will be advised that any requests for information are for research purposes only and that any inquiries by the MCCS will not be construed as a representation that a contract will be awarded.

3001. <u>RESPONSIBILITY OF THE REQUESTING ACTIVITY</u>. Determining requirements is the responsibility of the requesting activity or user. It is not a function of contracting personnel. The requesting activity will determine which supplies or services most adequately meet its needs and must clearly define those supplies or services on the purchase request. Specifications, purchase descriptions, and statements of work will be as precise as possible without unduly restricting competition. Where technical specifications are required, assistance may be obtained from the contracting office.

3002. <u>PURCHASE REQUEST/REQUISITION</u>. The requesting activity will forward their requirements to the contracting office on a purchase request/requisition. The purchase request/requisition will describe the supplies or services required, identify any recommended sources, indicate the amount budgeted for the procurement, the requesting activity's cost center, and the account number the purchase action will be charged to. It must certify that funds are available and that all required approvals have been obtained. Receipt of the purchase request/requisition in the contracting office begins the procurement process.

3003. <u>AVAILABILITY AND CERTIFICATION OF FUNDS</u>

1. The availability of funds for non-Exchange resale procurements will be ensured either through the electronic purchasing system approval process or certification on a paper purchase request (including requests for contract extension or modification). Contracting officers and purchasing agents are prohibited from making purchases when funding is insufficient. If for any reason the originally certified funds become insufficient, additional funds must be certified as available from the requesting office before the purchase order or contract can be awarded or modified.

2. Other instruments such as Indefinite-Delivery type contracts, Basic Ordering Agreements (BOA's), and Blanket Purchase Agreements (BPA's) may be established

prior to obtaining funding. Funds availability, however, will be certified prior to placing an order against these agreements.

3. Certification of funds availability is not required for the purchase of resale merchandise.

3004. <u>LEAD TIME</u>

1. Requesting activities will make every effort to establish a realistic delivery date in order that the purchase can be properly accomplished. Purchase requests will be submitted to the contracting office in sufficient time to allow for the procurement process to be completed, production time, and delivery of the supplies or services by the required delivery date.

2. Contracts awarded after contract performance has commenced subject MCCS to numerous liability issues and will be avoided. If the contracting officer permits performance to begin prior to contract award, the circumstances leading to this situation and the contracting officer's justification for the late award will be documented in the contract award memorandum. To avoid this occurrence, a Letter Contract may be negotiated (see paragraph 5321).

3005. <u>CONTRACTS VS PURCHASE ORDERS</u>. The administrative cost of establishing and administrating two-party (bilateral) contracts is not warranted for much of the equipment, supplies, and merchandise purchased by MCCS. The preferred method of procurement will be by purchase order, delivery order, or purchase card (see paragraph 6400).

1. Purchase Orders/Delivery Orders will be used for the following:

    a. Purchase of commercial equipment, supplies, and support services;

    b. Purchase of raw food products not supplied under a blanket purchase agreement or contract;

    c. Orders against existing NAF or other Government agency contracts;

    d. Customer Special Orders.

2. Bilateral contracts will be established for purchases of equipment, supplies, and services under the following circumstance:

    a. When the items or services require detailed specifications, statements of work, performance standards, drawings, or special provisions;

    b. When it is a revenue-generating concession, vending, or agency contract;

    c. When a contract is desirable or needed to ensure product availability during periods of shortages, or to guarantee firm prices for the contract period;

    d. When an Indefinite-Delivery contract is needed or desirable;

    e. When for any other reason the contracting officer determines that a bilateral negotiated contract rather than a unilateral purchase order would best serve MCCS interests.

3. Resale items may be purchased by purchase order, delivery order, or bilateral contract.

3006. <u>SPECIFICATIONS</u>

1. Specifications, including statements of work and purchase descriptions, will not be so restrictive as to improperly eliminate competition. Since specifications must be understood by both parties, industry-developed specifications should be used when possible.

2. In the event of a dispute between the contractor and the MCCS concerning ambiguous specifications, it is a general contract law principle that the specification ambiguity will be construed against the drafter, usually the MCCS. It is therefore imperative that specifications be clear and that all sections of a contract be consistent with each other in order to effect timely and economical procurements.

3007. <u>INSURANCE REQUIREMENTS</u>

1. When determined by the contracting officer, contractors will be required to carry insurance in amounts sufficient to protect the interest of the MCCS NAFI and the United States.

2. The contractor must provide a copy of the required Certificate of Insurance to the contracting officer prior to beginning performance.

3. Due to the nature of some contracted MCCS activities, additional insurance may be required. To determine the amount of additional insurance, MCCS will consider the following circumstances:

    a. The type of contract and the risks associated with the requirement (i.e., circuses, carnivals, aerobics, martial arts);

    b. Whether Government or MCCS property is involved (i.e., beauty and barber shop concessions);

    c. Whether the contractor has coverage for the specific type of business and the amount is acceptable to the MCCS;

    d. Whether the MCCS elects to assume the risks and/or obtain the type of insurance coverage required.

4. Questions concerning types and amounts of insurance will be forwarded to CMC(MR).

3008. <u>BONDS</u>

1. Performance bonds may be used for other than construction to protect the MCCS's interest when one or more of the following apply:

    a. MCCS property or funds are to be provided to the contractor for use in performing the contract or as partial compensation (i.e., when advance payment or startup costs are provided);

    b. Substantial progress payments are made before delivery of end items start;

    c. Contracts are for dismantling, demolition, or removal of improvements.

2. The contractor will furnish all bonds before receiving a notice to proceed with the work.

3. No bond will be required after the contract has been awarded if it was not specifically required in the contract, except as may be determined necessary for a contract modification.

3009. <u>CMC(MR) CONTRACTING OFFICE</u>. Contracting and purchasing personnel at CMC(MR) are available to assist MCCS procurement offices with procurement policy guidance, sample specifications/work statements, evaluation criteria, etc.

3010. <u>APPROPRIATED FUND CONTRACTING OFFICE</u>. MCCS procurement personnel are encouraged to request the assistance of installation appropriated fund contracting personnel on source list development, local vendor information, etc.

MCCS NAF PROCUREMENT POLICY

CHAPTER 4

PROCUREMENT SOURCES

CHAPTER 4

PROCUREMENT SOURCES

4000. MANDATORY SOURCES

1. Federal Prison Industries. The Federal Prison Industries (FPI), also referred to as UNICOR, is a mandatory source of products listed in the Schedule of Products made in Federal Penal and Correctional Institutions at prices not to exceed current market prices. Purchase from FPI is not mandatory and a waiver is not required if the Contracting Officer makes a determination that the FPI product or service is not comparable to supplies available from the private sector that best meet MCCS needs in terms of price, quality, and time of delivery; the supplies are acquired and used outside the United States; acquiring listed items totaling $2500 or less; or; acquiring services. The following procedures will be followed prior to purchasing products listed in the FPI Schedule:

    a. Conduct market research to determine whether the FPI item is comparable to products or services available from the private sector that best meet MCCS needs in terms of price, quality, and time of delivery. This is a unilateral determination made at the discretion of the contracting officer.

    b. Prepare a written determination that includes supporting rationale explaining the assessment of price, quality, and time of delivery, based on the results of market research comparing the FPI item to products or services available from the private sector.

    c. If the FPI item is comparable, purchase the item from FPI following the ordering procedures at http://www.unicor.gov, unless a waiver is obtained. Requests for waivers to purchase supplies or services listed in the FPI Schedule from another source shall be processed in accordance with the procedures as http://www.unicor.gov.

    d. If the FPI item is not comparable in one or more of the areas of price, quality, and time of delivery:

        (1) Acquire the item using competitive procedures.

        (2) Include FPI in the solicitation process and consider a timely offer from FPI for award in accordance with the requirements and evaluation factors in the solicitation.

2. National Industries for the Blind (NIB) and National Industries for the Severely Handicapped (NISH). The Government, to include military NAFIs, is required to purchase products (commodities) and services, if they are available within the period required, from sources on the "Procurement List". The Committee for Purchase from People Who Are Blind or Severely Disabled (the Committee) is an independent Federal agency that administers the Javits-Wagner-O'Day (JWOD) program and publishes the Procurement List. Additions to and deletions from the Procurement List are published in the Federal Register as they are approved by the Committee. (Public Law 92-28, 85 Stat. 77 (1971), as amended, 41 U.S.C. 46-48c, and 41 C.F.R. Ch. 51).

a. The Procurement List identifies the item designation for each commodity, including military resale commodities, and any limitation on the portion of the commodity that must be procured under the JWOD Act. "Military resale commodities" are those sold for the private, individual use of authorized patrons of commissaries and exchanges, or like activities of other Government departments and agencies.

b. When identical commodities or services are on the Procurement List and the Schedule of Products issued by Federal Prison Industries, Inc., ordering activities will purchase supplies and services in the following priorities:

    (1) Commodities:

        (a) Federal Prison Industries, Inc. (41 U.S.C. 48).

        (b) JWOD participating nonprofit agencies.

        (c) Commercial sources.

    (2) Services:

        (a) JWOD participating nonprofit agencies.

        (b) Federal Prison Industries, Inc.

        (c) Commercial Sources

c. The "Procurement List" may be obtained at http://www.jwod.gov/jwod/index.html.

4001. SMALL BUSINESS ACT. The provisions of the Small Business Act (15 U.S.C. Section 631 et seq.) do not apply to NAF acquisitions. Small business, small disadvantaged business, and minority business concerns will be encouraged to compete for MCCS requirements.

4002. U.S. GOVERNMENT SOURCES

1. Other Government activities, both appropriated fund and NAF, are authorized sources for goods and services. The agencies that may be in position to supply MCCS requirements include but are not limited to the General Services Administration (GSA) at www.gsa.gov, Defense Logistics Agency (DLA), Defense Personnel Support Center (DPSC), Defense Commissary Agency (DeCA), and other military exchange services and Morale, Welfare and Recreation (MWR) activities. GSA and DeCA will not be used as a source for resale items.

2. Per 10 U.S.C. Section 2482(a), MCCS NAFIs may enter into a contract or other agreement with another element of the DoD or other Federal department, agency, or instrumentality to provide or obtain goods and services beneficial to the MCCS NAFI. Consult MCCS Counsel for additional guidance.

4003. AIR FORCE NONAPPROPRIATED PURCHASING OFFICE

1. A Memorandum of Agreement (MOA) authorizes the Marine Corps MCCS to participate in Air Force Nonappropriated Fund Purchasing Office (AFNAFPO) programs. AFNAFPO invites all DoD NAFI's to participate in consolidated DoD - wide procurements. AFNAFPO obtains low prices by dealing directly with the manufacturer. Through volume purchasing of common need items, significant savings can be achieved.

2. MCCS procurement offices will contact AFNAFPO directly to request a list of their procurement programs and copies of their catalogs. Requests will be mailed to AFNAF Purchasing Office, 9504 IH 35 North, Suite 370, San Antonio, TX, 78233-6636. Inquiries may be directed to (800)722-3623 or http://www.afnafpo.com.

3. Each MCCS will issue its own delivery order for the product desired per the terms of the AFNAFPO contract. Delivery orders placed against AFNAFPO contracts or negotiated on behalf of the MCCS by AFNAFPO satisfy Marine Corps requirements for competitive NAF purchasing. If a problem develops with an order, the MCCS activity will make the initial contact with the vendor to try and resolve the issue. If the vendor fails to respond, the MCCS will contact the appropriate AFNAFPO contracting officer for assistance.

4004. COOPERATIVE EFFORTS. MCCS activities are encouraged to combine their requirements and to enter into local or regional contracts. These consolidated buys help reduce costs and standardize products throughout the Marine Corps.

1. To the maximum extent possible, contracting officers will include contract clauses in their contracts that permit other MCCS activities to participate in their contracts. Each MCCS activity will fund and place individual delivery orders against these contracts.

2. In addition to informal cooperative agreements, the MCCS also has Memorandums of Agreement (MOA) with fellow NAFI exchange and MWR organizations that allow us to participate in selected contracts. Where the MOA has been designated as mandatory, the MCCS will participate. MOAs may be negotiated at the MCCS level, or directed by CMC(MR) and forwarded to the appropriate MCCS activities.

4005. COMMERCIAL SOURCES. MCCS policy is to purchase standard commercial products readily available in commercial trade whenever feasible. Purchasing of standard commercial products does not normally involve development of specifications. Specifications will only be used when determined necessary to establish quality standards as a basis for competition when brand is not a factor. Specifications or purchase descriptions that establish minimum quality standards may also be used in the purchase of food, except when brand-name products may be justified. When specifications are needed, performance specifications are preferred over manufacturing specifications.

4006. PURCHASING ALCOHOLIC BEVERAGES

1. Alcoholic beverages purchased for resale (either through Exchange retail or Club operations) in the continental United States will be bought from the most competitive source and distributed in the most economical manner, price and other factors considered, except that:

a. Malt beverages and wine will be purchased from, and delivery accepted from, a source located in the same State as the military installation.

b. If the military installation, located in the continental United States, is located in more than one State, the purchase of malt beverages and wine may be made from a source of supply in either State.

2. Under Federal law (10 U.S.C. Section 2488) all alcoholic beverages purchased for military resale in Alaska and Hawaii will be purchased from in-state sources.

3. The types of alcoholic beverages purchased for military resale (either through Exchange retail or Club operations) is determined by market share of specific brands. Single source negotiation will be conducted with the approved distributors for the supply of the desired items to MCCS.

4. The U.S. alcoholic beverage industry is highly regulated with the production, distribution and sale governed by Federal and State laws and regulations. Questions concerning the purchase or resale of alcoholic beverages will be referred to MCCS Counsel.

4007. PURCHASING FROM OTHER THAN PRIME SOURCE

1. MCCS activities will purchase from the prime source when possible, unless industry practice deems it more appropriate to purchase from vendor representative firms. Factors to consider include, but are not limited to, a comparison of prices, minimum reorder quantities, distribution, freight terms, reduction in MCCS administrative and operational expense, and delivery time.

2. Procurement from vendor representative firms may be necessary to obtain the following services:

a. Information on new products, coming promotions, product knowledge, etc;

b. Shelf counts, shelf stocking, and rotation of merchandise;

c. Authorization for return of damaged or dated merchandise;

d. Training sales personnel, and providing product demonstrations and displays.

4008. BUY AMERICAN ACT. The Buy American Act (10 U.S.C. Section 2533a) requires that DoD acquisitions over the simplified acquisition threshold, currently $100,000, must be grown, reprocessed, reused, or produced in the United States or its possessions. It is applicable to the purchase of food, supplies or equipment for use by MCCS. The Buy American Act does not apply to:

1. Purchases outside the United States;

2. Purchases for resale in exchanges, commissaries, or other DoD NAFIs (Public Law 107-107, Title VIII, sec 832, DoD Authorization Act of 2002 and the Bery Amendment, 10 U.S.C. Section 2533a(g)).

4009. <u>DOD INTERNATIONAL BALANCE OF PAYMENTS PROGRAM</u>. The DoD International Balance of Payments Program (IBOP)(often referred to as the Gold Flow Program) applies to the purchase of foreign goods and services outside the United States, its possessions and Puerto Rico. See DoDD 7060.3 for IBOP procedures.

4010. <u>TRADE AGREEMENTS ACT</u>. The Trade Agreements Act (19 U.S.C. Section 2501 et seq.) exempts products of designated countries from the application of the Buy American Act in acquisitions over certain dollar thresholds.

1. The Act does not apply to:

    a. Purchases of resale merchandise;

    b. Purchases from Federal Prison Industries or from Nonprofit Agencies Employing People Who Are Blind or Severely Disabled.

2. The Act does apply to the purchase goods and services equal to or exceeding $175,000, and construction contracts equal to or exceeding $6,725,000.

3. The above dollar thresholds are adjusted approximately every two years to reflect the value of the U.S. dollar against the currencies of other nations. These thresholds are published in the Federal Register.

4011. <u>NORTH AMERICAN FREE TRADE AGREEMENT ACT</u>. The North American Free Trade Agreement Act (NAFTA) (19 U.S.C. Section 3301) exempts products from Canada and Mexico from the application of the Buy American Act in acquisitions over certain dollar thresholds.

1. The Act does not apply to:

    a. Purchases of resale merchandise;

    b. Purchases from Federal Prison Industries or from Nonprofit Agencies Employing People Who Are Blind or Severely Disabled.

2. The Act does apply to:

    a. Canadian supplies and services equal to or exceeding $25,000;

    b. Mexican supplies sand services equal to or exceeding $58,550;

    c. Construction contracts equal to or exceeding $7,611,532.

3. The above dollar thresholds are adjusted approximately every two years to reflect the value of the U.S. dollar against the currencies of other nations. These thresholds are published in the Federal Register.

4012. <u>FOREIGN SOURCES</u>

1. Contracting officers will not purchase any items that cannot be lawfully imported into the United States because of governmental restrictions, such as counterfeit trademarked items or copyright limitations on trade names.

2. Services and construction requirements at locations outside the United States may be negotiated with eligible sources consistent with host-country laws, treaties, or status of forces agreements.

3. MCCS activities located outside the United States will, within the limits of sound business practice, stock merchandise of U.S. origin in preference to equivalent merchandise from foreign sources.

4. Questions concerning purchasing jurisdiction in foreign areas will be forwarded to MCCS Counsel.

4013. PURCHASES OF FOREIGN GOODS IN THE UNITED STATES

1. Purchases in the U.S. of duty-paid foreign goods physically located in the U.S. are authorized. Importers having an exclusive franchise for distribution in the U.S. of foreign items are considered the prime source for these items.

2. A tax "drawback" will be applied for, when applicable. Drawback is a refund of U.S. customs duty paid on goods imported and later exported; for example, when a contractor imports sugar for a product that is later exported to overseas activities. The contract should include a tax drawback provision. In such cases, the contractor agrees to process claims for drawback of customs duty or refund Federal excise tax and to remit proceeds, less the cost of processing the claim, to MCCS. Contracting officers may use drawback information (amount of duty paid) to compute the cost of an item excluding duty.

4014. TRADEMARK ITEMS. U.S. registered trademarked items will be bought directly from trademark owners or from authorized, designated or franchised distributors. MCCS will not buy and sell counterfeit items bearing registered trademark logos.

4015. SOURCE FILES

1. Source files are required for items or services purchased by competitive solicitation. Source files are not required to purchase brand-name products from prime sources.

2. Names of sources may be developed from the internet, trade publications, associations, interviews, telephone directories, Chambers of Commerce, Small Business Administration, Minority Business Development Agencies, other NAFI or Government purchasing offices, the Thomas Register of American Manufacturers at (www.thomaspublishing.com), and other directories of association members.

4016. SOURCE LISTS

1. A source list is required for each competitive solicitation. It is developed prior to each solicitation from the source files and is retained in the solicitation file. The source list will contain a reasonable number of eligible sources to ensure adequate competition. Determining a reasonable number of sources is a contracting officer's judgment decision. It is based on the dollar amount of the purchase, competitiveness of the market, and number of interested offerors. There is no requirement to solicit all available sources for each purchase.

2. Always solicit an incumbent contractor unless the incumbent has clearly indicated no interest, becomes ineligible, or had a default termination on the prior contract. In that case, the defaulting contractor may be given the solicitation only on specific request.

3. State licensing agencies that provide rehabilitation services to the blind and other handicapped may, upon request, be placed on source lists to receive solicitations for services. See paragraph 5205 for applicability of Randolph-Sheppard Act requirements to contracts for non-Exchange vending and cafeteria operations.

4. Minority Business Development Agencies (MBDA), or firms they identify, should be placed on appropriate source lists if requested.

4017. INELIGIBLE SOURCES. MCCS requirements will not be purchased from individuals or firms who:

1. Are on the GSA publication "Lists of Parties Excluded from Federal Procurement or Nonprocurement Programs" (www.epls.gov), or on similar lists of offshore suppliers published by installation commanders.

2. Are active duty military personnel or civilian employees of the Government, unless the contracting officer determines there is no potential for or apparent conflict of interest. Contracting officers may also use immediate family members of military personnel or MCCS employees as sources if there is no potential for or apparent conflict of interest. In making this determination, contracting officers will consider the position of the individual, any relationship with MCCS, and the potential for the appearance of favoritism or undue influence. Solicitation and contract files will be documented to show the contracting officer's determination. MCCS Counsel will be consulted in questionable situations. MCCS may not award contracts to MCCS or military personnel to perform the same work under contract as they perform for MCCS in their MCCS or military position.

4018. REMOVAL OF SOURCES FROM SOURCE LISTS. Firms or individuals in a source file or on a source list who are later debarred or suspended, or who are otherwise determined to be ineligible, will be removed from source files and lists to the extent required by such debarment, suspension, or other determination of ineligibility.

CHAPTER 5

CONTRACT TYPES

CHAPTER 5

CONTRACT TYPES

5000. <u>GENERAL</u>. A contract defines the legal rights and obligations of the contracting parties. Contracts may, under specified conditions, be established on simple documents such as purchase orders, or they may be complex in nature, containing detailed specifications and performance standards. The following must be present for a valid contract: Competent parties, legal subject matter, legal consideration, mutual agreement, and mutual obligation.

5001. <u>CONTRACT TYPES</u>

1. MCCS will enter into fixed-price type contracts; MCCS will not enter into cost-reimbursement contracts without the prior approval of CMC(MR). MCCS fixed price contracts will be established by written purchase order, delivery order, or contract. The selection of the type of contract and the purchasing procedure to be used in a particular situation will be determined by the contracting officer.

2. MCCS contracts may also be described as Exchange and non-Exchange contracts. This distinction is important for legal jurisdiction over contract disputes. The Contract Disputes Act applies to Exchange contracts and subjects MCCS to the jurisdiction of federal courts during contract disputes. Non-exchange contracts are not subject to federal court jurisdiction and should not be drafted in such a manner as to imply such jurisdiction. See paragraph 7108 for additional guidance.

CHAPTER 5

CONTRACT TYPES

SECTION 1: EQUIPMENT, SUPPLY, AND MERCHANDISE CONTRACTS

5100. GENERAL. This section primarily addresses contracts for off-the-shelf commercial equipment, supplies, and merchandise that are purchased for use or resale of the MCCS. An off-the-shelf item is produced and placed in stock by a supplier before orders are received. Much of the following, however, is also applicable to the section on consumable items. Purchases of equipment, supplies, merchandise, and consumables should be made through an electronic purchase system, unless the complexity of the procurement or length of contract period requires negotiation of a two-party contract.

5101. INSPECTIONS. The NAF contracting officer or purchasing agent will ensure that equipment, supply, and merchandise contracts contain a clause giving MCCS the right to inspect and accept or reject items in order to ensure that MCCS receives exactly what it purchased. The extent of the inspection depends upon the item being inspected. The inspection should be thorough enough to determine whether the item conforms to the specifications.

5102. DEFECTS. Defects in the product can constitute grounds for rejection of the item. Patent defects, such as items damaged in shipment or items with parts clearly missing, are generally evident upon first visual inspection. Latent defects are not often evident upon first visual inspection and may not be noted until after the item has been accepted and paid for. If an inspection cannot be performed upon receipt, the receiving ticket should be noted "received and accepted pending inspection". A full inspection should be accomplished promptly in order to ensure that any defects are reported to the contractor within a reasonable period of time. A prompt inspection should also reveal concealed damage that was not evident upon initial receipt. Any defects or damages noted will be reported to the contracting officer immediately to allow the contracting officer to reject the items and to require corrective action.

5103. NONCONFORMING ITEMS

1. Nonconforming items are not necessarily defective. For example, a product in a 12-ounce bottle is ordered, but 24-ounce bottles are delivered. Accepting nonconforming items is discouraged but not prohibited, and the contracting officer is responsible for their acceptance or rejection. In determining whether to accept or reject them, the contacting officer will base his or her decision on the following:

    a. An explanation as to how the item nonconforms to specifications and how extensive the nonconformance is;

    b. Advice from the receiving activity on whether the item is acceptable to use and will perform its intended function;

c. A recommendation from the receiving activity (with supporting documentation) on whether to accept or reject the item;

d. The nature and extent of the contractual adjustment that will result from either decision.

2. If the decision is made to accept the item, the contracting officer will seek an equitable adjustment in the price of the item and negotiate any other adjustments necessary as a result of acceptance. If the decision is made to reject the item, the contracting officer will so notify the contractor and give the contractor the opportunity to correct the problem within the required delivery schedule.

5104. REJECTION PROCEDURES. The contracting officer will notify the contractor promptly in writing when items are being rejected, giving the reasons for the rejection. Whenever any items are rejected, the contract file will be documented to reflect that a rejection occurred, the basis on which the items were rejected (i.e. nonconforming or defective items), and the corrective action taken.

5105. ACCEPTANCE. Once items have been accepted, the acceptance is considered final (unless otherwise provided in the contract) except for latent defects, fraud, or gross mistakes amounting to fraud. Consequently, once the MCCS has accepted the shipment, it cannot be rejected later unless the acceptance can be voided because of one of these exceptions. If a defective or nonconforming item is not rejected within the time provided for in the contract or in the absence of such a provision, within a reasonable amount of time, MCCS is considered to have accepted it.

5106. RECEIVING REPORTS

1. Upon receipt, inspection and acceptance of goods and services, the receiving activity will prepare a receiving report for all goods received and services performed. The receiving report must contain the name and signature of the receiving person, and the date received and accepted. Receiving reports will be forwarded to the MCCS finance office and retained with the invoice document.

2. When goods and services are received as a result of an Open Purchase Order, Blanket Purchase Agreement call, or a utility services-type contract, receiving activities may utilize the vendor's delivery ticket or invoice as the receiving report document. Receiving activities will review the delivery ticket or invoice to ensure that it accurately reflects the quantity, quality, and pricing data of the goods and services ordered and received.

3. Activities using electronic purchasing systems will enter receipt of goods and services into the system.

5107. RETURNING EXCESS EQUIPMENT, SUPPLIES, OR MERCHANDISE. Unless provided for in the contract, if excess equipment, supplies, or merchandise is ordered MCCS has no contractual right to return the excess, unless it is defective or nonconforming to contract requirements. This does not prevent MCCS from negotiating with a contractor for the return of excess items.

5108. <u>WARRANTIES</u>

1. The requiring activities are responsible for monitoring warranties to ensure that when a repair or service is required, the warranty is invoked. Contracting officers will ensure warranty provisions and clauses are incorporated in contracts. In addition, contractors will be required to provide copies of warranties associated with the procurement of services, supplies and construction. When the supplier requires that forms be returned in order to enforce the warranty, the requiring activities will complete and return.

2. The basic remedy provided under a typical warranty clause requires the contractor to replace or correct defective supplies, or to reduce the price if the MCCS wishes to keep the supplies without correction or replacement. If MCCS requires correction or replacement, any transportation charges involved will be borne by the contractor. If MCCS decides to keep the items without correction, an appropriate equitable adjustment will be sought.

3. Contracting officers will not agree to contractor proposed open-ended indemnity clauses. Consult MCCS Counsel for guidance.

5109. <u>ONE-TIME-BUYS</u>. A one-time-buy is defined as a nonrecurring purchase of resale items not regularly carried. Examples include items for promotional purposes, seasonal requirements, emergencies because of shortages or non-availability of regular stock, or to satisfy unique requirements of command, military or Government sponsored programs. The term "one-time-buy" doesn't limit the purchase to a single purchase order or single source. The requirement may involve more than one delivery destination or multiple suppliers.

5110. <u>GUARANTEED SALES CONTRACTS</u>

1. A purchase on a guaranteed sale is a purchase where MCCS receives resale items into inventory and the contractor agrees to accept returns for credit all unsold quantities after a set period. Guaranteed sales contracts may be used for short-term promotions such as sidewalk/truckload sales and in addition for the following items or categories.

    a. Periodicals, books, maps, hobby items, sporting goods, sunglasses, seasonal items, etc.

    b. Products that expire and have date codes, such as packaged food items, medicine and vitamins, when guaranteed sales are the industry practice.

    c. Other items or other circumstances as authorized by CMC(MR).

2. Each contract awarded for guaranteed sale will provide that the contractor agrees to accept the return of unsold quantities by a specified date, for reimbursement or credit at the option of MCCS. Title to the merchandise initially passes to MCCS under the prescribed FOB terms in the contract. However, the contract should specify that when returns are made, title (and risk of loss) pass back to the contractor. Transportation and handling costs for returning items to the contractor will be negotiated by the purchasing agent before contract award and incorporated into the contract. Normally, the contractor is responsible for return

costs. Before awarding a contract on a guaranteed-sale basis and before starting a return, the purchasing agent must insure the contractor is financially capable of repaying MCCS for items returned under the guaranteed sale provision. The purchasing agent is responsible for insuring that items are returned by the specified date and that a request is made to the contractor for reimbursement or credit.

5111. <u>PURCHASES ON CONSIGNMENT</u>. A purchase on consignment is a purchase where the contractor retains title to the merchandise until it is sold. Title first passes to MCCS and then to the customer at the time of sale. MCCS pays the contractor for the quantities sold.

5112. <u>INDEFINITE DELIVERY, INDEFINITE QUANTITY (IDIQ) CONTRACTS</u>. Indefinite delivery contracts are used when the exact times and/or exact quantities of future deliveries are not known at the time of award. There are three types of these contracts: indefinite quantity, definite quantity, and requirements. These contracts are often referred to as (IDIQ) contracts. Delivery orders placed against these contracts must be within the scope, issued within the period of performance, and be within the maximum value of the contract.

1. Indefinite-quantity contracts provide for an indefinite quantity, within stated limits, of supplies or services during a fixed period. Individual delivery orders are placed against the contract when quantities are defined. A minimum order amount must be specified in the solicitation and resulting award, as well as the maximum the contractor is expected to provide.

2. Definite-quantity contracts provide for a definite quantity, within stated limits, of supplies or services during a fixed period when delivery times and destinations cannot be predetermined. Individual delivery orders are placed against the contract as they are identified.

3. A requirements contract provides for the filling of all actual purchase requirements of designated supplies or services with one provider during the specified period. Individual orders are placed against the contract for deliveries or performance. The estimated quantity is not a representation to the offeror that the estimated supplies or services will be required or ordered. Requirements contracts are primarily used when faster delivery of production items is required, as the contractor is usually willing to maintain limited stocks when the MCCS will obtain all of its actual purchase requirements from the specified source.

5113. <u>LEASE OR PURCHASE OF EQUIPMENT</u>

1. It is frequently more economical to acquire certain equipment by short-term lease rather than by purchase. A service contract format will be used for equipment leases. The decision to lease rather than to purchase must be made on a case-by-case basis, applying the following criteria:

    a. The MCCS need is short-term or intermittent, and purchase would be costlier than leasing;

    b. It is likely that the equipment will become obsolete within a short period and replacement will become necessary;

c. The lessor will provide the equipment, as well as maintenance and repair service, at a price lower than would otherwise be available through an outright purchase.

2. Documentation as to the rationale used for lease versus purchase will be retained in the contract file.

5114. CAPITAL LEASES. MCCS activities are authorized to enter into capital leases. For a lease to be classified as a capital lease versus an operating lease or rental contract, the agreement must meet any one of the following criteria:

1. The lease transfers ownership of the equipment to the MCCS by the end of the lease term.

2. The lease term is equal to 75 percent or more of the estimated economic life of the leased equipment.

3. The lease contains a bargain purchase provision allowing MCCS, at its option, to purchase the leased equipment for a price that is sufficiently lower than the expected fair market value of the item. This option is made known at the inception of the lease.

CHAPTER 5

CONTRACT TYPES

SECTION 2: CONSUMABLES AND SUBSISTENCE CONTRACTS

5200. <u>GENERAL</u>

1. Consumable items are products that lose their identity during use or are consumed during the course of daily business. These are classified as non-edible items. Consumable items include, but are not limited to, paper products, fuel, postage stamps, and airline tickets.

2. Subsistence includes all food and beverage items. These are classified as edible or drinkable items.

5201. <u>SUBSISTENCE FOOD PROCUREMENT</u>. Specifications for subsistence food items will be written per generally accepted industry standards. While it is important to define exactly what is needed, the specifications should not be so stringent as to limit the choice of suppliers. For meat products, the Institutional Meat Purchase Specifications (IMPS), and the National Association of Meat Purveyors (NAMPS), approved by the United States Department of Agriculture (USDA), are generally sufficient.

5202. <u>FOOD SOURCES</u>. "The Directory of Sanitarily Approved Food Establishments for Armed Forces Procurement (In CONUS)" is published under provisions of NAVSUPINST 4355.4F and MCO P10110.31G and lists establishments that have been approved by Headquarters, U.S. Army Health Services Command, as processors of food procured for the Armed Forces. A copy of this Directory may be obtained by writing the U.S. Army Health Services Command, Fort Sam Houston, Texas 78234-6000, or calling DSN 471-6510 or (210) 221-6510. A complete listing of approved commercial sources should be available through installation veterinarians, or website: http://vets.amedd.army.mil/vetcom. Questions concerning approved food sources may be forwarded to the installation PMO or veterinary representative. Sources which indicate interest in doing business with MCCS, and which are not on the approved list, should be encouraged to apply for approval.

5203. <u>FOOD INSPECTIONS</u>

1. All food processing and sanitation on Marine Corps installations, whether a direct or indirect (contract) operation, will comply with the requirements of NAVMED P-5010-1, Manual of Naval Preventative Medicine. (www/vnh.org/PreventiveMedicine/PreventiveMedicine.html). Contracting officers will include this requirement in all MCCS contracts for food services. To ensure compliance, food service activities are subject to random inspection by the installation Veterinary Service representative. The decision with respect to the wholesomeness and acceptability of food products, as well as food storage, preparation, and disposal procedures, the cleanliness of food service spaces, equipment, and utensils, and the medical screening of food service personnel, remains with the military veterinary officer. In the event of a conflict between

the NAVMED, any relevant Marine Corps Order, or the contractor's own food
processing and sanitation requirements, the NAVMED P-5010-1 will take precedence,
unless one of the others is more stringent.

2. When a wholesomeness problem not creating an imminent health hazard is reported
by the MCCS food facility manager or installation veterinary representative, the
contracting officer will immediately send a cure letter to the contractor
requesting corrective action be taken within 10 calendar days and to provide a
report of the actions taken. If the contractor's action is considered inadequate
as evidenced by subsequent veterinary reports, a show-cause letter will be
initiated by the contracting officer and followed by contract termination if
appropriate.

3. Whenever a veterinary inspector reports that fresh dairy food(s) create or
appear to create an imminent health hazard, the contracting officer will
immediately issue a cure letter to the contractor. The letter will state that
corrective action is required within 24 hours, or within three (3) calendar days of
receipt of the notice, depending on type of health hazard. Should the contractor
fail to take the designated action, the contracting officer will issue a show-cause
letter, followed by contract termination if appropriate for those item(s) creating
or appearing to create an imminent health hazard. Emergency purchases from another
approved source can be made during the period deliveries cannot be accepted from a
contractor.

4. Contract personnel employed in MCCS food facilities will comply with
introductory and annual food service sanitation and food safety training
requirements specified in NAVMED P-5010-1. The resulting Food Safety Training
Certificate (NAVMED 4061/1) will be retained on site at the food facility.

5204. BRAND NAME RETAIL FOOD PRODUCTS

1. MCCS activities may stock and sell brand-name food items. Requirements are
generally based on customer preference and/or demand and therefore require no
formal competition, however competition will be obtained when the brand name is
available from multiple sources.

2. The conditions established above for purchasing institutional food products
from approved sources and related sanitary and wholesomeness requirements apply to
purchasing retail food items. Brand name food manufacturers or distributors will
notify MCCS activities if food products are recalled.

5205. RANDOLPH-SHEPPARD ACT. The Randolph-Sheppard Vending Stand Act (20 U.S.C.
Section 107) requires that a priority be given to the blind in the establishment of
contracted non-Exchange vending and cafeteria operations on federal property.
Contact CMC(MR) for additional guidance.

CHAPTER 5

CONTRACT TYPES

SECTION 3: SERVICE CONTRACTING

5300. <u>GENERAL</u>. A service contract is a contract that directly engages the time and effort of a contractor whose primary purpose is to perform an identifiable task rather than to furnish an end item of supply. A service contract can cover services performed by either professional or nonprofessional personnel and can be performed by an individual or an organization. Services operations may sell ancillary products similar to those sold in commercial firms. If product sales are permitted, the contract will include this requirement (or option) and address product pricing.

5301. <u>PERSONAL AND NONPERSONAL SERVICES CONTRACTS</u>

1. A nonpersonal services contract is a contract under which the personnel rendering the services are not subject, either by the contract terms or by the manner of its administration, to the supervision and control of the MCCS/Government.

2. A personal services contract is a contract that, by its express terms or as administered, makes the contractor personnel appear, in effect, as MCCS/Government employees. MCCS may not enter into personal services contracts unless specifically authorized to do so. Questions regarding personal service contracts will be forwarded to MCCS Counsel.

3. To ensure that nonpersonal service contracts do not become personal service contracts by the manner of its administration, MCCS will adhere to the following:

    a. Contracts shall not be used for performance of "inherently governmental functions." An "inherently governmental function" is one so closely related to the public interest as to mandate performance by Government employees. These functions imply the use of Government discretion or authority, or the making of decisions on behalf of the Government.

    b. All contractor personnel attending meetings, answering MCCS telephones, and working in other situations where their contractor status is not obvious to third parties are required to identify themselves as such to avoid creating an impression in the minds of members of the public and any non-MCCS officials or employees that they are MCCS officials or employees.

    c. All documents and reports produced by contractor personnel will be marked as contractor products or ensure that contractor participation is appropriately disclosed.

5302. <u>CONTRACT PERSONNEL REQUIREMENTS</u>. MCCS contractors and their employees performing tasks and services in the United States must be U. S. Citizens or lawfully admitted aliens for permanent residence. Questions regarding personnel requirements will be directed to MCCS Counsel; questions concerning specific contract personnel will be directed to the installation security office.

5303. <u>SERVICE CONTRACT ACT OF 1965</u>

1. The Service Contract Act of 1965 (41 USC 351 through 358, as amended) requires that contractors pay not less than prevailing wages and fringe benefits and provide safe conditions of work under contracts for the performance of services in the US through the use of service employees.

2. The Service Contract Act (SCA) applies to service contracts that exceed $2500. Prevailing wage rates are established by the Department of Labor (DoL) upon receipt of a Standard Form 98 and 98a, "Notice of Intention to Make a Service Contract and Response to Notice" from a contracting officer. The contracting officer will request a wage determination for each new contract and extension to an existing contract. Copies of applicable Collective Bargaining Agreements (CBA) will also be submitted to the DoL. Refer to Department of Labor, Wage and Hour Division, web site for more information at http://www.dol.gov/esa/public/whd.

3. The DoL Wage and Hour Administrator will issue wage determinations in response to the Notice of Intention if the Act applies. The contracting officer will include the wage determinations in solicitations and existing contracts (via contract modification) every two years through the life of the contract. Where a CBA is in place the DoL will require the contractor to comply with it.

4. The SCA is applicable to support service contracts (such as janitorial, landscaping, maintenance, etc) and to revenue generating service contracts (such as concession, vending, special events, etc). The SCA also has special requirements for service contracts where the contract employees receive tips from patrons.

5. The SCA is not applicable to contracts with companies of less than five employees, contracts for professional, consultant or administrative services, and contracts for construction. There are other exemptions from the Act contained in 41 U.S.C. Sec. 356. If a wage determination or CBA is not applicable to the MCCS contract, employees of the contractor are required to be paid not less than minimum wage under the Fair Labor Standards Act.

6. Questions regarding the applicability or implementation of the SCA will be directed to Counsel or CMC(MR).

5304. <u>LABOR DISPUTES</u>. When a labor dispute arises between a contractor and the contractor's employees, MCCS personnel will remain impartial and will refrain from the conciliation, mediation, or arbitration of any such dispute. MCCS personnel will cooperate, and encourage contractors to cooperate, with Federal and State agencies responsible for enforcing requirements concerning safety, health, and sanitation; maximum hours and minimum wages; equal pay for equal work; child and convict labor; and equal employment opportunity. The contracting officer will require the contractor to report any ongoing or potential labor dispute that might have an impact on delivery or performance.

5305. <u>EQUAL EMPLOYMENT OPPORTUNITY (EEO) REQUIREMENTS</u>. The EEO provisions of Executive Order 11246, as amended, will be included in contracts over $10,000 per year in the U.S. For contracts and each contract modification of $10,000,000 or more, a pre-award clearance must be obtained. Contact CMC(MR) for additional guidance.

5306. MCCS USE OF PRIVATE SECTOR TEMPORARIES

1. Contracting officers may enter into contracts or basic ordering agreements with temporary help service firms for the brief or intermittent use of the skills of private sector temporaries consistent with the regulatory requirements contained in 5 CFR Part 300 Subpart E. Services furnished by temporary help firms will not be regarded or treated as personal services. These services will not be used in lieu of regular recruitment under MCCS direct-hire practices or to displace an MCCS employee. The NAF contracting officer will require the activity to submit a statement giving the circumstances of the project for which the short-term services are needed. For any extension beyond the initial period of services, an exception must be obtained from the supporting personnel office. The personnel officer will determine whether a direct-hire is the appropriate method versus temporary services.

2. An exception to the above term limit is granted at overseas locations when authorized in the Status of Forces Agreement.

5307. INDIVIDUAL SERVICE CONTRACTS

1. An Individual Service Contract (ISC) is a nonpersonal services contract where payment is made on a per job or per student/patron basis. ISCs are for temporary or intermittent requirements of less than one year; examples include arts and crafts or aerobics instructors.

2. MCCS activities may contract with MCCS employees and enlisted active duty members for individual services, such as recreational instructors and entertainers, when no conflicts of interest exist and it is necessary to obtain the services of an individual with unique skills, experience, or knowledge.

3. Contracts with individuals are not subject to the Service Contract Act (paragraph 5302). Refer to paragraph 2016 for contractor tax requirements.

5308. PROFESSIONAL AND CONSULTANT SERVICES. Professional services are provided by members of a recognized profession, such as accounting or engineering. Consulting services are those of a purely advisory nature. Professional and consultant services are provided by persons and/or organizations that have knowledge and special abilities not generally available within the MCCS.

1. Using professional and consultant services is a legitimate way to improve MCCS services and operations. These services are used to help managers achieve maximum effectiveness or economy in their operations.

2. The MCCS may not contract for professional or consultant services:

    a. To perform work of a policy-making, decision-making, or managerial nature that is the direct responsibility of MCCS officials; or

    b. To bypass or undermine personnel ceilings, pay limitations, or competitive employment procedures.

3. The contracting officer is responsible for determining whether the requested contractual action, regardless of dollar value, is for professional or consultant

services. Before processing any contractual action for these services, the
contracting officer will ensure that the required documentation is complete and
included in the contract file. Questions concerning such contracts will be
referred to MCCS Counsel.

4. MCCS may not contract for legal services without express authorization from the
Counsel for the Commandant (CL), HQMC. Such requests must be submitted with
justification through the regional MCCS Counsel and CMC(MR).

5309. SPORTS PROFESSIONALS. The services of sports professionals (i.e., golf,
tennis, ski) may be obtained by direct-hire NAF employment or by professional
service contract when determined to be in the best interest of the MCCS.
Negotiation of contracts for sports professionals may be conducted on a limited or
single source basis if it is documented:

1. The professional's competence, such as teaching ability, past accomplishments,
and technical expertise is of greater importance than price or fee considerations,
and;

2. There are a limited number of professionals with the technical expertise to
meet MCCS needs.

5310. ENTERTAINMENT CONTRACTS. Contracts for entertainment will be solicited and
awarded based on the following criteria:

1. The popularity of the entertainers and/or groups, patron preference,
availability, participatory draw, profit margin, and past performance. These types
of contracts are considered revenue-generating contracts when awarded on a
percentage basis. When booking entertainment, the use of an entertainment agency
is encouraged when feasible.

2. Since an entertainer is usually available through only one agent, and because
the selection is based in large part on customer preference, competition is
generally not required. Where there is more than one agent who can provide
entertainment of equivalent quality at comparable prices in a given geographical
area, the use of available agents will be rotated.

5311. SPECIAL EVENTS

1. Carnivals, circuses, rodeos, and similar events require advance approval from
the installation commander, or designee, in writing. Requirements for installation
support, such as law enforcement, first aid, and traffic control personnel, will be
documented in advance of the event.

2. Since operators of these events often schedule their bookings months in
advance, solicitation planning should begin eight to twelve-months in advance of
the desired event date(s). To determine contractor responsibility, the contracting
officer will require a minimum of three references from each offeror. References
from a public institution, such as a county government are preferred. Prior to
award, the police department of the city or county where the offeror recently
performed should be contacted for information on safety issues such as property
damage, personal injuries, and control of money.

3. Special event contracts will identify types and number of rides, acts, exhibits, or games, and ticket prices or fees charged. Contracting officers will ensure special events with potentially unsafe practices, such as riding devices, animal shows, or food sales, meet applicable safety and sanitation requirements. Contracts shall include provisions to indemnify the MCCS and U.S. Government.

4. Recurring special events will be competitively solicited and awarded via multi-year contracts (i.e. a one-year contract with four one-year renewal options, or a three or five year contract specifying events in alternating years).

5. The Service Contract Act is applicable to providers of special events, and its provisions will be included in special event contracts. Entertainment and short-term commodity sales concessions, held in conjunction with special events, will comply with requirements of paragraphs 5308 and 5320.

6. Air Shows are command-sponsored events and as such should be funded by appropriated funds; however, most air shows have a significant MCCS NAF component, (concessions, entertainment, runway events, golf tournaments, etc.) which support the command event. MCCS contracts issued to support air shows will be coordinated with the air show point of contact.

5312. <u>INTERIOR DESIGN REQUIREMENTS</u>

1. To preserve the integrity of the design process, procurements for all interior and kitchen design requirements, regardless of whether design was done in-house or by contract (i.e., Architect-Engineer or interior design firm) will not be competed. In addition, interior design packages that are specified as part of a construction project will also not be competed. The contracting officer is encouraged to negotiate contract terms, conditions and pricing.

2. Items specified for purchase may be procured without further comparison or substitution, unless such a substitution is due to non-availability, and is first approved by the designer.

3. Interior designers developing an office design will consider office furniture manufactured by the Federal Prison Industries (FPI). Should FPI products be considered acceptable, for purposes of the design, a market survey will be conducted to ensure that the FPI products are comparable to the private sector in price, quality, and delivery. The designer will include a memorandum of record detailing the considerations given the FPI products and the basis of the decision if FPI products are not incorporated in the design.

4. A market survey for purchase of office furniture not a part of a design package will be accomplished prior to purchase. If it is determined that an FPI product is not comparable in price, quality and delivery to the private sector product, the product will be acquired competitively and FPI given the opportunity to compete.

5313. <u>MAINTENANCE CONTRACTS</u>. Facilities maintenance contracts cover the upkeep of MCCS facilities (buildings, grounds, and interior facilities) or the regular care and reconditioning of MCCS tools and equipment (including but not limited to computers, typewriters, photocopy machines, forklifts, etc.). NAF maintenance contracts are service contracts and are awarded when appropriated fund monies or support is not authorized. Services such as routine building/grounds maintenance and equipment/systems maintenance may also be contracted.

5314. <u>CONSTRUCTION CONTRACTING</u>. All MCCS facilities construction, repair, and maintenance projects will be coordinated with the installation Public Works Officer prior to execution.

1. MCCS NAF construction requirements may be accomplished by the MCCS contracting officer if granted a special delegation of construction contracting authority by the Naval Facilities Engineering Command (NAVFAC).

2. If a delegation of construction contracting authority has not been issued, MCCS requirements exceeding $2,000 will be forwarded to the installation Officer-In-Charge (OIC) or Resident-Officer-In-Charge of Construction (ROICC) for procurement action, or to an activity with NAF construction contracting authority.

3. Construction contracts over $2,000 are subject to the Davis-Bacon Act, which requires prevailing wage rates that must be paid to laborers and mechanics employed by contractors and subcontractors working on public works and buildings.

4. MCCS contracting officers and purchasing agents may contract for minor repair or maintenance projects up to $2,000.

5315. <u>PATRON SERVICE CONTRACTS</u>. These revenue-generating contracts involve contractor sale of goods and services to authorized patrons within the military community. (Non-revenue generating service contracts, by contrast, normally provide a service to the MCCS, it is not sold directly to the military community, and the MCCS pays the contractor). Patron service contracts are designed to ensure contractor-operated activities provide the desired level of customer service. To do this, various types of contracts are used. The concession contract is the most common; others include vending, agency, and short-term commodity sales contracts.

5316. <u>CONCESSION CONTRACTS</u>

1. Concession contracts grant a concessionaire the right to sell selected items or to provide a specific service in a designated location for a specific period of time. The actual work may be done inside the MCCS facility or outside the military installation, or a combination of the two.

2. In concession contracts the contractor (concessionaire) pays a fee to MCCS. Commissions from concession contracts will be based on a percentage of sales. Concession contracts are usually awarded for a minimum of one year, and are generally subject to the Service Contract Act.

5317. <u>PATRON SERVICE TEST CONTRACTS</u>

1. Patron service test contracts may be negotiated on a noncompetitive basis when a potential concessionaire presents a unique patron service operation to the MCCS. If the MCCS is unsure of the business viability of the operation, a one-year or lesser term test contract may be negotiated.

2. The purpose of the contract is to test the feasibility and profitability of the operation for both the MCCS and the concessionaire. If after one year the test is successful based on patron response and return to MCCS, the MCCS will:

     a. Competitively solicit the service and award any follow-on contract using standard procurement practices, or;

     b. Choose to operate the service on a direct basis.

3. If the contract is not successful MCCS will cancel the requirement.

4. The contracting officer will determine offeror responsibility and price reasonableness prior to award of the test contract. Findings will be documented in the Justification for Award memorandum. The contract will state the contract period is limited to one year.

5. MCCS Counsel will review all patron service test contracts prior to award.

5318. <u>DIRECT PATRON CONTACT</u>. Solicitations and resulting contracts for concession services with direct patron contact (i.e., barber, beauty, optical) will include:

1. Whether the operators will be required to have state licenses and/or certificates of training;

2. Specific sanitation requirements concerning the use of clean brushes, towels, etc.;

3. Procedures for handling customers who have communicable diseases (such as scalp irritation).

5319. <u>VENDING CONTRACTS</u>. Vending contracts are similar to concession contracts in that they also generate revenue and are subject to the Service Contract Act, although many large vending firms have Collective Bargaining Agreements in place.

1. Under a standard Vending Contract for food and beverage items, the MCCS owns the vending machines and competes the product cost. The prices of the items vended are determined by MCCS, and are not a factor in negotiations with the contractor. The contractor may be required to restock the vending machines, or deliver the product to a central MCCS location where it is restocked by MCCS personnel.

2. Under a Vending Machine Rental and Service contract, MCCS rents machines, purchases restocking services, and buys a product from the contractor. MCCS sets the prices of the items vended. Competition is on the product cost and machine rental and service charge.

3. Contracts for video and arcade games, as well as "kidee rides", are usually similar to Vending Machine Rental and Service Contracts (unless the machine is owned by the MCCS). Contracts for rented machines will specify the frequency of machine rotation.

5320. AGENCY CONTRACTS. In an agency contract, MCCS acts for or represents the contractor in a transaction with the customer. The contractor is the principal, and MCCS is the agent. MCCS accepts patron orders for services or items on behalf of the contractor who then fills the order. In some cases, MCCS may rent the contractor's items to the patron. In both cases, the MCCS accepts payment from the patron. MCCS liability is limited to that of an agent. MCCS will not contract to perform any obligations of the principal. MCCS forwards monies and taxes collected minus commission to the contractor. The commission to MCCS will be competed in agency contracts. Agency contracts will be considered an indirect operation for MCCS reporting purposes.

5321. LETTER CONTRACTS. If failure to award a contract by a specific date will result in the loss of MCCS property or assets, a Letter Contract may be negotiated. A Letter Contract authorizes the contractor to begin performance prior to award of the standard contract. It is signed by the contracting officer and contractor, must specify the maximum liability of MCCS; and must indicate the time period in which the contract will be definitized (awarded by a standard contract). Letter Contracts will be avoided if another procurement instrument is available. Letter Contracts will be coordinated with Counsel prior to execution.

5322. SHORT TERM COMMODITY SALES/CONCESSIONS. This is a noncompetitive concession contract for the display and sale of merchandise from temporarily assigned space. It is primarily used for the sale of handicraft items and other merchandise customarily sold at craft fairs or in conjunction with promotional programs at commercial shopping centers and malls. These concessions generally operate for 15-30 days or less; however, the contract may be negotiated for intermittent or regularly scheduled periods during a one-year period. Concessions offering the same or similar commodities will be rotated. Item restrictions and cost price limitations applicable to Exchange retail facilities apply to commodity concessions. Refer to DoD Instruction 1330.21.

5323. CONCESSION CONTRACT REQUIREMENTS. In addition to the contract requirements listed at paragraph 2006, clauses concerning the following, regardless of the supply or service under contract, will be included in each concession contract. Most of these requirements are also applicable to vending, agency, and short-term commodity sales concession contracts:

1. Service Contract Act Wage Determination, when applicable;

2. Identify the commission as a percentage of total sales, and the method and time of payment;

3. Require the concessionaire to conspicuously post a price list for all goods or services available. The concessionaire must adhere to the prices specified;

4. Require the concessionaire to furnish cash registers or similar business machines, and or pre-numbered sales slips approved by the activity manager, or that the concessionaire use equipment and or sales slips furnished by the MCCS;

5. Require the concessionaire to keep complete and accurate records of all transactions and to ring all sales in the customer's view;

6. Identify reports that the concessionaire must provide to the MCCS;

7. Require the concessionaire to safeguard all assets in his or her possession in which the MCCS or the Government has an interest;

8. Require the concessionaire to certify the integrity of his or her financial records and reports;

9. Provide MCCS the authority to audit or inspect (or to have audited or inspected) the records, premises, and operations of the concessionaire for the purpose of ensuring contract compliance;

10. Require separate physical inventories to be taken of all MCCS and Government owned equipment at the time that the concessionaire occupies the premises and annually thereafter, and on the final day of contract performance;

11. Notice of veterinary inspection when food products are sold in the activity (Refer to paragraph 5203).

5324. CONTRACTOR FINANCED BUILDING IMPROVEMENTS. If the contractor is required to provide the capital for improvements to the contractor-operated facility, the commission payment to MCCS may be lower than if the contractor does not incur these costs. If this option is chosen, the solicitation will clearly state what improvements are required. The MCCS activity will assist the contractor in obtaining all required command approvals.

5325. CONTRACTOR CAPITAL INVESTMENT

1. Revenue generating service contracts requiring contractor capital investment will normally not exceed a contract period of five (5) years. A contract period of up to 25 years may be considered, if the contractor's capital investment:

    a. Is largely unrecoverable at the end of a five (5) year contract period (i.e., contractor-financed construction or renovation of Government property); and

    b. Is of such magnitude that a longer period is necessary to allow reasonable return to MCCS and the contractor, and is consistent with industry amortization standards.

2. MCCS activities having a requirement that meets the above criteria will document the basis for their decision. The supporting payback analysis will be retained in the contract file.

3. All contracts with a contract period in excess of five (5) years will receive MCCS Counsel review and approval prior to award. Approval documentation will be retained in the contract file.

5326. PUBLIC - PRIVATE VENTURES (PPVs). PPVs offer an alternative source of funding for large capital projects, and must be considered prior to investment of NAF funds. MCCS activities will follow the procedure in SECNAVINST 7010.7 for review and approval. Upon contract award, the PPV contractor may provide a portion or all of the financing, design, construction, services or facilities to the MCCS.

5327. <u>INSTALLATION SUPPORT AGREEMENTS</u>. In certain situations the MCCS may provide support services (i.e. maintenance, grounds keeping, food services) to the installation. Agreements of this type will be reviewed and approved by MCCS Counsel prior to award.

5328. <u>INFORMATION TECHNOLOGY</u>

1. Requirements for the procurement of Information Technology (IT)hardware, software, or support systems will be coordinated with CMC(MR) to determine compatibility with existing systems and the MCCS network.

2. Contracting officers will request a complete copy of the company warranty and software licensing agreement as part of the offeror's proposal. IT license, support, and services agreements will receive close review to ensure they are in compliance with MCCS contract clauses. IT contracts or agreements which require MCCS to sign the contractor's form will be reviewed by MCCS Counsel prior to signature by the contracting officer.

MCCS NAF PROCUREMENT POLICY

CHAPTER 6

NEGOTIATED PROCUREMENT

SECTION 1: RETAIL BUYING

SECTION 4: PURCHASE CARD

CHAPTER 6

NEGOTIATED PROCUREMENT

6000. <u>CONDUCTING NEGOTIATED PROCUREMENT</u>. MCCS procurement is accomplished by competitive negotiation. The manner in which MCCS conducts its business with industry directly shapes its image and reputation in the business community. Negotiation with suppliers will be consistent with these guidelines: obtain the best possible prices, terms and conditions that are fair to the seller, giving consideration to the cost factors of both MCCS and the supplier, and is in the best interest of MCCS. It may be appropriate to consider factors such as the effect on future negotiations, maintenance of sources of supply, incentives to good performance, and performance under unique circumstances.

6001. <u>RESPONSIBILITY</u>

1. Responsibility refers to an offeror's ability to perform a contract. No MCCS contract or purchase order may be awarded to any person or firm unless the contracting officer determines that the prospective contractor is responsible within the meaning of this paragraph. A determination of responsibility is made prior to the time of award. To be considered responsible, the potential contractor must:

    a. Have adequate financial resources;

    b. Be able to meet the proposed delivery or performance schedule;

    c. Have a satisfactory performance record;

    d. Be otherwise qualified and eligible to receive an award under applicable laws and regulations.

2. For each procurement over $5,000, the contracting officer's determination of responsibility will be documented and retained in the contract file. For simple procurement actions this determination may be made on the Record of Negotiations (MCCS Form 401-R). For complex procurement actions (i.e., a revenue generating or multi-year contract), this determination will be documented in the Justification for Award memorandum.

3. When a negative responsibility determination is made against a prospective contractor, a written determination of nonresponsibility will be prepared, signed by the contracting officer, and retained in the contract file. Documented reasons must be included in any determination of nonresponsibility. The contracting officer will coordinate all proposed determinations of nonresponsibility with MCCS Counsel.

4. To assist in determining an offeror's responsibility, written solicitations for multi-year contracts will be accompanied by a request for a financial statement. Solicitations for multi-year revenue-generating contracts will also request a projected operating statement.

6002. <u>SOURCES OF INFORMATION REGARDING RESPONSIBILITY</u>

1. Information on prospective contractors may be obtained from the following sources:

     a. The GSA publication, Lists of Parties Excluded from Federal Procurement or Nonprocurement Programs (http://www.ARNET.gov/epls);

     b. The prospective contractor;

     c. Existing information within the DoD including records on file and knowledge within the activity making the purchase, other purchasing offices, or other NAF activities;

     d. Dunn and Bradstreet reports;

     e. Other sources including suppliers, subcontractors and customers of the prospective contractor; banks and financial institutions; commercial credit agencies; Government departments and agencies; purchasing and trade associations; Better Business Bureaus and Chambers of Commerce.

2. All information regarding prospective contractors must be put in writing, the source of information identified and retained in the contract file.

6003. <u>FAIR AND REASONABLE PRICE DETERMINATION</u>

1. MCCS contracts and purchase orders will include a fair and reasonable price determination based on the following considerations:

     a. Price is acceptable to the buyer and to the seller;

     b. Price is competitive with other vendors providing similar products or services;

     c. Price is not excessive for the time that delivery is required or that the service be performed;

     d. Cost of administering the purchase is not excessive.

2. For each non-resale procurement over $5,000, the contracting officer's determination of fair and reasonable pricing will be documented and retained in the contract file. For simple procurement actions, this documentation may be made on the Record of Negotiations Form (MCCS Form 401-R). For complex procurement actions (i.e., revenue generating or multi-year contracts), this determination will be documented in the Justification for Award memorandum.

3. The Robinson-Patman Act (15 U.S.C. Section 13) prohibits vendors from discriminating among their commercial customers by offering different prices to different customers for commodities of like quality and grade (other factors being equal, i.e. quantity, date of delivery, etc.). However, it is not applicable to the U.S. Government. Therefore, vendors may legally negotiate lower prices with MCCS activities than what they offer to their commercial customers. Evidence of

the contractor's prices being equal to or lower than those offered to commercial customers (other factors being equal) will be used to document price reasonableness.

6004. COMPETITION THRESHOLD

1. The preferred method of MCCS procurement is by requesting quotations or soliciting proposals from multiple sources. However, the following requirements may be solicited from only one source if the price is determined fair and reasonable, and:

   a. The requirement is for a brand-name resale item;

   b. The purchase is for packaged beverages to be obtained from the franchised distributor in the area;

   c. The estimated cost of equipment, supplies, or services is below the competition threshold (currently $5,000). See paragraph 5303 for applicable Service Contract Act requirements;

   d. When no competitive interest is apparent in contracts for services, including revenue-generating services, having average monthly sales of $2,500 or less;

   e. When contracting for short-term commodity sales concessions (see paragraph 5322);

   f. When the purchase is made from a prescribed mandatory source such as the Federal Prison Industries (FPI), the National Industries for the Blind (NIB) or the National Industries for the Severely Handicapped (NISH);

   g. When the purchase is made from a source that has already met the competition requirement, such as AFNAFPO or GSA;

   h. When negotiating for the purchase of training requirements up to $25,000, providing:

       (1) Training courses will be commercially available through a regular dealer;

       (2) Prices are determined fair and reasonable;

       (3) Training managers must document their reasons for selecting training sources, regularly survey the market to ensure MCCS obtains the best value for their training programs, and rotate training sources as appropriate.

   i. When the purchase is in support of a cooperative effort with other DoD NAFIs and has been approved by the Director, CMC(MR);

   j. When the purchase is made from a nonprofit institution or federally funded research and development center.

2. Under no circumstances will a requirement be split to avoid contracting procedures or competition requirements.

6005. NONCOMPETITIVE PROCUREMENT. Noncompetitive procurement is a contract for the purchase of supplies or services after negotiating with only one source.

1. Competition is not required when the supplies or services are only available from a sole source, the source is determined responsible, and no other type of supplies or services will satisfy MCCS requirements. Such determination will be based on the following:

    a. MCCS's minimum needs can only be satisfied by unique supplies, services, or capabilities available from one source, and no other types or sources of supplies or services will satisfy MCCS requirements; or

    b. The items or services are protected by limited rights in data, patents, copyrights, secret processes, trade secrets, or other proprietary restrictions, and are available only from the originating source; or

    c. The requester has determined that only specified brands or models of equipment, components, or accessories, or only specific academic or professional credentials will satisfy the requirement; or

    d. The requirement is for unique repair or replacement parts for existing equipment for which substitutions cannot be made; or

    e. Access to such utility services as electric power or energy, gas (natural or manufactured), water, cable or satellite television or other utility services, is restricted by local law, custom, or availability, and only one supplier can furnish the service within that geographical area; or when the contemplated contract is for construction of a part of a utility system and the local utility company is the only source available to work on the system.

    f. Supplies or services may be considered to be available from only one source if the source has submitted an unsolicited proposal (see paragraph 6012).

2. Supplies or services are also exempt from competition when there is reasonable justification to conclude that MCCS minimum needs can only be satisfied by one single source, as a result of:

    a. The specific performance, technical, functional or aesthetic characteristics of a particular brand, model, or style of supplies or services is unavailable from another source;

    b. The added cost to the MCCS of duplicating design or development efforts already performed by the source selected;

    c. The added cost to the MCCS of training, briefing, or otherwise educating an alternate source on the progress of the project or program in which the source selected has already participated;

    d. The documented inability of other potential sources to meet the stated delivery requirements;

    e. The unique credentials of a firm or other technical consultant or expert.

3. Noncompetitive procurement actions must be justified as required in paragraph 6006.

6006. JUSTIFICATION FOR NONCOMPETITIVE PROCUREMENT ACTIONS

1. A contracting officer will not commence negotiations for noncompetitive procurements, unless he or she:

    a. Ensures technical personnel and requiring activities provide documentation to support their recommendation for noncompetitive procurement;

    b. Ensures the justification contains sufficient facts and rationale to justify noncompetitive procurement.

2. For each procurement action over $5,000, the contracting officer's justification for noncompetitive procurement, including follow-on noncompetitive procurement actions, will be documented and retained in the contract file. For simple procurement actions, this justification may be made on the Record of Negotiations (MCCS Form 401-R). For complex procurement actions (i.e. contracts for revenue-generating services or multi-year contracts), this justification will be documented in the Justification for Award memorandum.

3. Given the fact that the majority of MCCS procurements involve commercial off-the-shelf equipment and supplies, noncompetitive procurements will be discouraged.

6007. FOLLOW-ON NONCOMPETITIVE PROCUREMENT REQUIREMENTS

1. Equipment and supplies may be deemed to be available only from the original source in the case of a follow-on contract for continued development or production (for example, additional units, replacement items, or for integration with existing systems) when it is likely that award to any other source would result in:

    a. Substantial duplication of cost to MCCS that is not expected to be recovered through competition;

    b. Unacceptable delays in fulfilling MCCS requirements.

2. Services may be deemed to be available only from the original source in the case of follow-on contracts for the continued provision of highly specialized services, to include professional services, when it is likely that award to any other source would result in:

    a. Substantial duplication of cost to MCCS that is not expected to be recovered through competition;

    b. Unacceptable delays in fulfilling MCCS requirements.

3. In addition to the above, follow-on contracts for equipment, supplies, or services may be deemed available only from the original source when multiple quotations are not reasonably obtainable or when competitive negotiation is otherwise impractical.

4. Justification for follow-on noncompetitive procurement actions will comply with paragraph 6006 requirements.

6008. REQUESTS FOR QUOTATION

1. A request for quotation (RFQ) is a request for pricing and delivery data for the future purchase of standard commercial goods or services, and is used for informational purposes. A quotation is not an offer and cannot be accepted by the MCCS to form a binding contract. An order issued by a contracting officer or purchasing agent in response to a supplier's quotation does not establish a contract. The order is an offer by MCCS to the supplier to buy certain supplies or services upon specified terms and conditions and only becomes a contract when the supplier accepts the offer (usually by performance).

2. Orders for service requirements may not be issued if the requirement is subject to the Service Contract Act (Refer to paragraph 5303).

6009. TELEPHONIC REQUESTS FOR QUOTATION

1. As provided below, price quotations may be solicited over the phone if the equipment, supplies, or services to be purchased are simple enough to only require a price quote, and award is made by purchase order or delivery order. The purchasing agent will keep records of telephonic price quotations to show the basis of placing the order at the price paid with the supplier concerned. These records will consist of the date, names, and phone numbers of the suppliers contacted, the names of the persons quoting, the prices, and other applicable terms quoted by each. If time permits, an electronic or fax confirmation of each supplier's price quote should be requested.

2. Competitive requests for quotation via the telephone is authorized under the following conditions:

    a. Estimated cost of equipment or supplies is under $5,000; or

    b. Estimated cost is over $5,000 but under $10,000 for standard off-the-shelf items that can be easily identified and oral quotation involves only a price and delivery offer; or

    c. Quotations for prices against blanket purchase agreements for fresh meats and poultry, eggs, frozen products, fresh fruits and vegetables, and other food products; or

    d. Due to urgency, sufficient lead-time is not available to permit an electronic or mailed request for quotation for items over $10,000. In this case the requiring activity must document the short lead time in the purchase requisition.

6010. FACSIMILE (FAX) OR ELECTRONIC REQUESTS FOR QUOTATION

1.   Use of the facsimile (fax) machine or e-mail to issue electronic Requests for Quotation (RFQ) in writing is preferred over telephonic price quotes.

2. The RFQ faxed or e-mailed to each source, the price quotations and terms and conditions received from each offeror, and all cover sheets and receipt confirmation pages will be retained in the purchase file. All faxed or e-mailed

correspondence will clearly identify the date, company name, phone number, fax number or e-mail address, and the name of the individual submitting the fax or electronic quote. Negotiations between the purchasing agent and offeror(s) concerning the electronic RFQ will be documented and retained in the purchase file.

6011. MAILED REQUESTS FOR QUOTATION

1. Mailed requests for quotation may be used for any purchase action, and will be used when obtaining oral or electronic quotes is not considered economical or practicable (i.e., some companies will not give telephonic or electronic price quotes).

2. Published price lists, such as those provided with a vendor's catalog are considered to be mailed quotes. However, contracting personnel will contact the vendor to ensure price information is current and MCCS obtains the benefit of applicable discounts before placing an order.

6012. UNSOLICITED PROPOSALS

1. An unsolicited proposal is a written proposal submitted to the MCCS for the purpose of obtaining a contract with the MCCS and is not in response to a formal or informal request. Upon receipt, unsolicited proposals will be forwarded to the contracting officer for coordination, evaluation and disposition.

2. Advertising material, commercial product offers, or technical correspondence are not unsolicited proposals. An unsolicited proposal must:

    a. Be innovative and unique, and not generally available from a competitive source;

    b. Be independently originated and developed by the offeror;

    c. Be prepared without Government or MCCS input;

    d. Include sufficient detail so MCCS can determine if the service is worthwhile, and the proposed work could benefit the MCCS mission; and

    e. Does not resemble a pending competitive procurement requirement.

3. An unsolicited proposal will be evaluated based upon:

    a. The unique or innovative method, approach, or concept demonstrated by the proposal, and the potential benefit to the MCCS mission;

    b. The offeror's capabilities, related experience, and the qualifications of key personnel assigned to the project.

4. If the unsolicited proposal is determined acceptable for award without competition, the contracting officer and potential contractor will use the proposal as the basis for negotiation of price and terms.

5. Contracts for studies, analyses, or consulting services will not be entered into without competition on the basis of an unsolicited proposal without the prior approval of CMC(MR).

6. Unsolicited proposals will receive legal review prior to commencement of negotiations.

6013. <u>BUY-INS</u>

1. "Buying-in" refers to the practice of offerors trying to obtain a contract award by knowingly offering a price that is below or approximate to anticipated costs, or a fee that is so high as to preclude a reasonable return. MCCS policy does not prohibit buy-ins if performance of the contract will not be jeopardized. If a contract is awarded at a buy-in price or fee, the contracting officer will be alert to any inappropriate attempt to increase the contract price, lower the fee, substitute items or provide less service than that prescribed by the contract, or failure to deliver buy-in priced items.

2. When a price or fee appears unrealistic, the contracting officer will outline the actions taken and summarize the decision on why the offer was accepted in the Justification for Award memorandum.

6014. <u>ELECTRONIC COMMERCE</u>. Use of electronic commerce in executing purchase orders, delivery orders, and contracts is recommended for MCCS contracting officers and purchasing agents.

1. Electronic commerce is a paperless process including electronic mail, electronic bulletin boards, electronic funds transfer, electronic data interchange, and similar techniques accomplishing business transactions.

2. Electronic data interchange (EDI), is electronically transferring information between computers, using established and published formats and codes, as authorized by the applicable Federal Information Processing Standards (FIPS).

6015. <u>ELECTRONIC PURCHASE SYSTEM</u>. MCCS requiring activities, contracting officers, and purchasing agents will enter requisition, purchasing, and receiving actions into the CMC(MR) designated purchasing systems.

6016. <u>ELECTRONIC PURCHASE ORDERS</u>. MCCS contracting officers and purchasing agents will issue electronic unsigned purchase orders (EPO) as implemented by CMC(MR) automated purchasing systems.

1. Prior to execution of an unsigned EPO the following conditions must be met:

    a. It is acceptable to the supplier;

    b. It does not require written acceptance by the supplier;

    c. The contracting office retains all official contract administration functions.

2. When an unsigned EPO is used:

    a. Appropriate clauses will be incorporated by reference;

    b. Administrative information that is not needed by the supplier may be placed only on copies intended for internal distribution;

    c. The same distribution (electronic or hard copy) used for signed purchase orders will be used for the unsigned EPO; and

    d. If an electronic copy is retained, no hard (paper) copy of the purchase order form is required.

CHAPTER 6

NEGOTIATED PROCUREMENT

SECTION 1: RETAIL BUYING

6100. <u>ITEM SELECTION</u>

1. Insofar as practical, the selection of resale items should be comparable to practices and procedures in the commercial retail trade. Market research techniques include review of trade publications, attendance at trade shows, and vendor product presentations.

2. MCCS objective is to stock items and brands most in demand by customers. Broad consumer acceptance of an item in the commercial sector is adequate evidence of customer demand for the item to be stocked.

3. Products will be evaluated based on selection factors such as quality, price, consumer trends, customer acceptance, and past sales experience.

4. Eligible sources may present products for purchase consideration. Products will be evaluated on a fair and impartial basis along with all others. When products are not selected, if requested the vendor will be told the reasons why.

5. Merchandise for U.S. resale in MCCS activities will be limited to the items or categories and cost limitations authorized in the Armed Services Exchange Policy (see DOD Instruction 1330.21).

6101. <u>BRAND-NAME MERCHANDISE</u>. Because of the nature of the MCCS mission, most resale items will be purchased on a noncompetitive basis from the prime sources of brand-name products. Identification of brand name items in the stock assortment justifies noncompetitive purchase from the prime source.

6102. <u>NON BRAND-NAME MERCHANDISE</u>. Unless otherwise justified, competitive procedures will be used when buying non brand-name items. The resale items will be standard commercial products readily available in the retail trade.

6103. <u>SOCIAL RESPONSIBILITY AND LABOR STANDARDS</u>. Suppliers and manufacturers of private label merchandise, or manufacturers of merchandise imported directly by MCCS or MCCS subcontractors, will comply with Social Responsibility and Labor Standards requirements.

CHAPTER 6

NEGOTIATED PROCUREMENT

SECTION 2: PURCHASING

6200. GENERAL. This section applies to procurement actions made through the use of a purchase order or similar document. It is applicable to the purchase of equipment, supplies, merchandise and support services.

6201. PURCHASE ORDERS

1. A purchase order (PO) is a purchase instrument for the future delivery of equipment, supplies, merchandise or for the future performance of services. The contracting officer or purchasing agent will incorporate all contract clauses required for or applicable to the particular procurement. A PO obligates the MCCS to pay the supplier the amount stated on the purchase order, if the contractor performs in accordance with the terms and conditions of the purchase order.

    a. A unilateral purchase order is one that is signed only by the contracting officer or purchasing agent. It constitutes an offer by the MCCS to pay for the future delivery of supplies or performance of services and does not require written acceptance by the supplier. It gives the MCCS the opportunity to cancel the order at any time before the supplier initiates performance without liability to the MCCS. It does not, however, create a contract nor ensure that the supplier will perform in accordance with the terms of the order. When a unilateral telephone order is placed, a written order will be prepared and documented as a confirming order to avoid duplicate shipments. When a unilateral order is accepted by the supplier (usually by performance), the PO becomes a binding contract and may only be changed or terminated by modification.

    b. A bilateral purchase order is one that is signed by both the contracting officer or purchasing agent and the supplier. It creates a binding contract between the MCCS and supplier and cannot be changed or terminated without a written modification.

2. Direct Delivery Agreements, Open Purchase Orders, and Blanket Purchase Orders are bilateral purchase orders open for an extended period of time during which multiple product deliveries or the performance of services are scheduled. These purchase agreements are generally used for the purchase of resale merchandise and performance of related support services such as shelf stocking.

6202. UNPRICED PURCHASE ORDERS. An unpriced purchase order is an order for supplies or services, the price of which is not set at the time the purchase order is issued. Unpriced purchase orders will not be used when the price of an item or service is available. Unpriced purchase orders will only be used if the total anticipated (or actual) price of the transaction will not exceed $5,000 and it is impractical or impossible to obtain the exact price in advance (i.e., repair or maintenance services). The unpriced purchase order will specify a "Not To Exceed" amount. The necessity for use of an unpriced purchase order will be documented on the Record of Negotiations (MCCS Form 401-R).

6203. DELIVERY ORDERS

1. A delivery order (DO) is an order for the future delivery of equipment, supplies, merchandise or services, placed against an existing contract or agreement. It may be used for orders of any dollar amount. It obligates the MCCS to pay the supplier the amount on the DO, if it is placed per the terms and conditions of the basic contract, and if the supplier performs per the terms and conditions of the contract.

   a. Most DOs are placed against contracts awarded by the General Services Administration, other nonappropriated fund instrumentalities (such as the Air Force Nonappropriated Fund Purchasing Office (see Paragraph 4003)), and CMC(MR). Each DO will include the contract number that the DO is placed against.

   b. A task order is similar to a DO, but is an order for services (vs. for products) placed against an existing contract. For simplicity, the MCCS has elected to use the term delivery order for all orders placed against existing contracts.

2. Prior to issuing a DO, the contracting officer or purchasing agent will:

   a. Ensure the basic contract authorizes DOs to be placed against it.

   b. Review the prices, specifications, and terms of the basic contract, and all modifications to that contract, to ensure it will meet the needs of MCCS.

3. MCCS procurement personnel and/or the supplier may not change the prices, specifications, or terms of the basic contract. If such a change is desired, it must be requested from and negotiated by the original contracting office and the supplier. Once the basic contract has been modified, the MCCS contracting officer or purchasing agent may issue a DO against the contract, as modified.

6204. BASIC ORDERING AGREEMENTS(BOA)

1. A Basic Ordering Agreement (BOA) is a written document containing terms and conditions of performance that have been negotiated by the contracting officer and the supplier. It contains clauses that apply to future orders between the parties. It is not a contract in and of itself, but serves as a tool intended to simplify purchasing procedures. In addition, a BOA contains a description of the supplies or services to be covered under the agreement, their prices, and the method by which future orders may be issued.

2. A BOA may be used when precise requirements are not known but a significant number of requirements are expected to be purchased against the agreement. The BOA will contain no guarantees that purchases will be made against it and will not be used to restrict competition.

6205. BLANKET PURCHASE AGREEMENTS(BPA)

1. Blanket Purchase Agreements (BPAs) provide a simplified method of purchasing recurring requirements by establishing monthly charge accounts with qualified sources. BPAs reduce administrative costs since separate purchase orders and multiple payments are not necessary.

2. The contracting officer negotiates BPAs to provide sources of supply for MCCS activities. The BPA must include a list of the items or services furnished, dollar limitation of the orders that may be placed against it, and the names and/or job titles of the individuals authorized to place calls against the BPA. MCCS contracting officers designate individuals to serve as BPA callers per paragraph 6206.

3. To encourage competition, BPAs will be issued to more than one supplier for requirements of the same type. A BPA is complete when the purchases under it equal the amount funded or its term expires.

6206. <u>APPOINTMENT/DELEGATION OF BPA CALLERS OR ORDERING AGENTS</u>. MCCS contracting officers may appoint BPA callers or ordering agents who are authorized to place orders against blanket purchase orders or open purchase orders. These individuals may be delegated specific ordering authority by the contracting officer to place small dollar value orders against existing contracts. Appointments will be in writing and must specify the maximum dollar limitation on orders authorized against the agreement. Placement of individual orders in excess of $5,000 will be limited to contracting officers and purchasing agents acting within the limits of their authority. BPA callers and ordering agents may place individual orders of $5,000 or less.

6207. <u>EMERGENCY PURCHASE PROCEDURES</u>

1. Emergency purchases by personnel without a procurement warrant, or designation as a BPA caller or ordering agent, are authorized for emergency-type services or repairs or for purchase of goods that are needed immediately due to unforeseeable circumstances requiring immediate action. To be considered an emergency, such requirements cannot be obtained through the use of normal purchase procedures and the delay of action may cause destruction or loss of MCCS property or assets. Emergency purchase procedures will not be used to alleviate the need for prior planning or to circumvent normal procurement procedures.

2. Emergency purchase actions will be reported in full detail to the MCCS contracting office the next duty day after the emergency action. The contracting officer or purchasing agent will complete the procurement action by preparing an after the fact PO or DO. Documentation explaining the emergency procurement action will be retained in the purchase file. In the absence of valid emergency criteria and prompt formalization of the purchase, actions will be handled as unauthorized commitments and will be processed per Paragraph 1014 of this Manual.

CHAPTER 6

NEGOTIATED PROCUREMENT

SECTION 3: COMPETITIVE NEGOTIATION

6300. GENERAL. Competitive negotiation, as distinguished from sealed bidding, allows the contracting officer more flexibility in arriving at a fair and reasonable price and mutually-agreed-upon contract terms. Competitive negotiation is a method of contracting that involves soliciting proposals, receiving proposals without a public opening, and further negotiation to allow for revision of offers prior to contract award. Contract award may also be made from initial proposals received without further negotiation.

6301. SOLICITATION AND REQUEST FOR PROPOSALS(RFP)

1. A Request for Proposals (RFP) is a written solicitation that provides a potential contractor with the opportunity to offer a price and a plan for accomplishing a particular procurement action. RFP's are used in negotiated procurements to communicate MCCS requirements to prospective contractors and to solicit proposals to meet these requirements. RFP's will contain the information necessary to enable prospective contractors to prepare proposals properly. Solicitation provisions and contract clauses will be included in the solicitation or incorporated by reference. A proposal received in response to a RFP is an offer that may be accepted by MCCS to create a binding contract following negotiations.

2. By contrast, an Invitation for Bid (IFB), using sealed bid procedures, furnishes a requirement and potential contractors provide only prices. With an IFB, there is no opportunity for the bidder to negotiate the terms of the contract and no deviations from the terms of the IFB are allowed. IFB's are an appropriated fund procurement method and will not be used by MCCS activities.

3. RFPs may be used at the discretion of the contracting officer for any procurement, however, they will be used for:

    a. Support or patron service type contracts in excess of $2,500 and/or the Service Contract Act applies;

    b. Complex requirements, drawings and/or detailed specifications are involved.

4. Contracting officers will ensure identical information concerning the procurement action is furnished to all prospective offerors.

6302. SOURCE LIST DEVELOPMENT. To promote competition contracting officers will ensure an appropriate number of sources are solicited; the minimum number is three. Sources may be found in the local community, through industry websites, and business/trade associations. To achieve competition, contracting officers may advertise their requirement in a Government medium, such as FedBizOps or GSA eBuy, or through websites designed to promote commercial business opportunities.

6303. PRESOLICITATION NOTICES. If a source file is excessively long or if a solicitation is complex, the contracting officer may send a presolicitation notice to the firms in the source file to determine interest. Those indicating no interest, or failing to respond, will not be solicited. Responses to presolicitation notices will be retained in the contract file.

6304. SOLICITATION FORMAT. Contracting officers will prepare solicitations and resulting contracts using standard contract formats. Based on the complexity and estimated dollar volume of the contract, the contracting officer will select one of the following:

1. Basic Contract Format. This contract format will be used for simple procurement actions valued up to $25,000, and is recommended for two party contracts such as instructors, entertainment, and minor repair and maintenance. At a minimum, simple contract format will consist of: specifications or statement of work, price or fee schedule, contract period, mandatory contract clauses, signatures of both parties and date signed, and attachments as appropriate.

2. MCCS Contract Format. This format will be used for most revenue generating contracts and support service contracts. Contract sections will follow the specified format, as appropriate to the specific procurement action.

3. Uniform Contract Format. The Uniform Contract Format will be used for complex procurement actions or at the option of the contracting officer.

6305. CONTRACT CLAUSES

1. All MCCS contracts and purchase orders, despite the format used, require specific clauses be included. MCCS contracts will include the following mandatory clauses: Changes, Examination of Records, Dispute Resolution, and Terminations (see DoDD 4105.67).

2. All MCCS NAF contracts will identify the responsible NAFI, and will state that no appropriated funds of the U.S. will be obligated, due or payable to the contractor.

3. Federal law also mandates MCCS and our contractors comply with statutes such as the Buy American Act, Trade Agreements Act, Service Contract Act, etc., when applicable. Contracting officers and purchasing agents will ensure clauses supporting the necessary statutes are included in MCCS contracts.

6306. EVALUATION FACTORS. Factors considered in evaluating offers will be tailored to each procurement and include only those factors that will have an impact on selecting the source. Price or fee is a factor in all MCCS procurements, as is past performance and/or experience. Other evaluation factors that may apply are technical, management capability, personnel qualifications, and present ability to meet the performance schedule. Solicitations using complex evaluation techniques, such as Best value or weighted factors will receive legal review and concurrence prior to issuance.

6307. <u>SOLICIATION DISTRIBUTION</u>. The RFP and any subsequent amendments will be distributed as follows:

1. One complete copy will be sent to each offeror;

2. One complete copy will be retained in the contracting office;

3. One complete copy will be provided to the requesting activity. Prior to issuing the solicitation, the contracting officer will coordinate the RFP with the requesting activity and obtain their concurrence on whether the solicitation meets their needs.

6308. <u>AMENDMENTS</u>. After the solicitation has been issued, but before the closing date, it may become necessary to make changes to the solicitation. Such changes may include changes in quantity, specifications, or delivery schedule; correcting defects or ambiguities; or changing the closing date for receipt of proposals. Such changes will be made by issuing a solicitation amendment to all firms who were sent the original solicitation. Before issuing an amendment, the contracting officer will decide whether the closing date for receiving proposals needs to be extended and will coordinate this change with the requiring activity. Solicitation amendments with significant changes will be coordinated with MCCS Counsel.

6309. <u>SOLICITATION PROTESTS AND PROTEST APPEALS BEFORE AWARD</u>. Any interested party may forward a written objection to a solicitation. This objection is a Protest, and may be received either before or after award. Refer to paragraphs 7101 through 7105 for guidance.

6310. <u>TWO-STEP NEGOTIATION</u>

1. Two-step procurement procedures may be used for the purchase of services, equipment and supplies when specifications are inadequate for usual solicitation procedures.

2. The two-step procedure will be considered when all of the following conditions exist:

    a. Specifications or purchase descriptions are indefinite or incomplete, or are too restrictive; and

    b. Definite criteria exist for evaluating technical proposals and deciding which is to the best advantage of MCCS; and

    c. More than one technically qualified source is available; and

    d. Sufficient time is available for the two-step method.

3. Step one is getting unpriced technical proposals. After evaluating proposals, the contracting officer advises offerors if they're acceptable. The contracting officer may clarify or resolve related requirements such as management approach, facilities, or conformity to technical requirements; however, data related to the subsequent negotiation (step two) will not be discussed.

4. Step two is the single or multiple source negotiation with offerors submitting acceptable technical proposals.

5. Under the two-step negotiation method, technical expertise must be used to determine requirements, establish criteria for evaluation, and make the proposal evaluation.

6311. <u>PREPROPOSAL CONFERENCES</u>. Preproposal conferences may be used as a means of briefing prospective offerors after a solicitation has been issued but before offers are prepared. Generally, preproposal conferences are used in complex procurements to explain or clarify requirements. The preproposal conference will be conducted by the contracting officer; technical and legal personnel will attend as appropriate. All prospective offerors will be furnished identical information on the proposed procurement, regardless of whether or not they attend the conference. A complete record, including names, organizations, and mailing addresses of the conference attendees, will be prepared and retained in the contract file.

6312. <u>CLOSING DATE</u>. The specified date, time and time zone for receipt of proposals will be clearly stated in the solicitation. The time is computed from the date of mailing of the solicitations to the date set for the receipt of proposals.

6313. <u>RECEIPT OF PROPOSALS</u>

1. At each contracting office, one person and an alternate will be designated to receive and safeguard all proposals until opening. Proposals will remain unopened in their original envelopes and kept in a locked drawer, cabinet, or safe until the scheduled time and date of the official opening. Proposals will not be left unattended on desks, in mail trays or in work areas.

2. Proposals opened by mistake before the official opening will be resealed immediately and delivered to the person designated for receipt. The individual who opened the proposal will make a notation on the envelope indicating the circumstances.

6314. <u>OPENING PROPOSALS</u>

1. On or soon after the date and time specified for receipt of proposals, the contracting officer will open the proposals in the presence of two MCCS witnesses. The contracting officer will prepare a summary or abstract of proposals noting the time and date of receipt, the proposed price or fee, and any other pertinent information contained in the proposal. The summary will be signed by the contracting officer and witnesses, verifying the accuracy of the information it contains. Complex proposal data may be entered onto an electronic spreadsheet for further analysis and evaluation. The completed spreadsheet will be signed and dated in ink by the contracting officer and MCCS witnesses.

2. Fax proposals, electronic proposals, amended/confirmed proposals, and proposals submitted in response to requests for Best and Final Offers will be received in accordance with the above.

3. Prior to contract award the contracting officer will prepare a Justification for Award memorandum. Refer paragraph 6324.

6315. SAFEGUARDING PROPOSALS. After opening and recording proposals, the contracting officer is responsible for safeguarding proposals until contract award is made and ensure proposal data is released only to people having a need to know. Individuals performing review and approval of proposed awards must safeguard proposal data while in their possession. Before award, proposals and summaries or abstracts of proposals must be kept in a locked drawer, cabinet or safe at all times. If personnel not having a need to know have access to these spaces, the documents must be kept in sealed envelopes. Disclosure of proposal information to any unauthorized person before award of the contract is a violation of MCCS policy and business ethics and may subject the violator to disciplinary action.

6316. LATE PROPOSALS. A late proposal is defined as any proposal or amendment that is received after the time and date set in the solicitation for receipt of proposals. MCCS reserves the right to consider late proposals or late revisions to proposals when it would be to MCCS advantage to do so; however, late proposals will not be solicited nor encouraged.

1. Late proposals (including revisions) will be opened to determine if it would be to MCCS's advantage to consider them. A late proposal that results in a tie with the most competitive offer timely received will not be considered.

2. If a later proposal is received that displaces the most competitive timely proposal received, and it meets MCCS basic needs and offers lower prices or higher fees, it may be considered if it is technically acceptable. If so, all offerors who submitted technically acceptable proposals (including the late one) will be advised that a late proposal was received and is being considered. All offerors will be given the opportunity to revise their proposals via solicitation amendment procedures (Refer to paragraph 6307).

3. A late proposal or late revision should not be considered if it appears that the integrity of the competitive negotiation process might be jeopardized. Proposals that are substantially late (i.e., 2 days or more) are more likely to jeopardize the integrity of the process.

4. Late proposals and revisions of proposals not considered will be retained with other unsuccessful proposals.

6317. CANCELLATION OF SOLICITATIONS. A solicitation may be cancelled at any time before award when the contracting officer determines it is in the best interest of MCCS. All firms that submitted a proposal will be advised in writing (letter, fax, or solicitation amendment may be used) and all proposals will be returned. The Justification for Award memorandum will be destroyed. If a new solicitation is to be issued, the offerors will be advised in the cancellation notice. Offers received under the cancelled solicitation will not be disclosed.

6318. <u>DISCLOSURE OF PRE-AWARD PROPOSAL INFORMATION</u>. Information contained in any proposal will not be disclosed until after contract award. Limited information about the successful proposal may be released after contract award, and is usually limited to the contractor's name. Disclosure of other information will be coordinated with MCCS Counsel prior to release.

6319. <u>EVALUATION PANELS</u>. Complex, technical, or high dollar procurement actions may call for the establishment of an evaluation panel to assist the contracting officer in evaluating offeror proposals.

1. With the assistance of the requesting activity, the contracting officer will appoint several individuals to a technical or price evaluation panel. Panel members will be chosen based on their experience and understanding of the functional or technical requirements of the solicitation, their ability to analyze the proposed offers, and their integrity and understanding of the procurement process.

    a. Usually two or more representatives from the requesting activity will be appointed to the technical evaluation panel. Technical evaluation panel members may not review price proposals.

    b. If price proposals consist of unusual or complex pricing, the contracting officer may determine a price evaluation panel is necessary. The price evaluation panel usually consists of members with financial or business management experience. Price evaluation panel members may not review technical proposals.

    c. In addition to MCCS activity personnel, evaluation panel members may include installation representatives, or personnel from other MCCS, NAFI, or DOD activities.

    d. Evaluation panel members may not consist of individuals from the private sector.

    e. The contracting officer will not be a member of the evaluation panel.

2. To ensure the integrity of the procurement process, the contracting officer will prepare evaluation forms using the evaluation factors stated in the solicitation. A copy of the solicitation and evaluation form will be provided to the panel members. The contracting officer will instruct evaluation panel members on the evaluation process. Upon completion of their evaluation, panel members will submit documentation explaining their recommendation. The contracting officer may require evaluation panel members to reach a consensus decision, or require each member submit an individual recommendation without consultation of other panel members. In both cases, documentation supporting the recommendation will be signed and dated by each panel member, and will include all work papers used during the evaluation process.

3. Evaluation panel members may not divulge or discuss proposal data with anyone other than the contracting officer or other evaluation panel members.

4. The contracting officer will use the specified evaluation data in determining contract award, however the contracting officer is not required to follow panel recommendations. The contracting officer will document the findings of the

evaluation panel(s), and the basis for his or her decision, in the Justification for Award memorandum. Refer to paragraph 6325.

5. All evaluation panel recommendations and supporting documentation will be retained in the contract file.

6320. ORAL PRESENTATIONS

1. Oral presentations by offerors may be used to supplement written information. Use of oral presentations as a substitute for portions of a proposal can be effective in streamlining the source selection process. Oral presentations may occur at any time in the procurement process, and are subject to the same restrictions as written information, regarding timing and content. Oral presentations provide an opportunity for dialogue among the parties in competitive, single, and sole source acquisitions.

2. Oral presentations usually provide the methods that prospective offerors will use, and allow for questions and answers. Oral presentations may also allow the evaluation panel members to speak directly with the personnel who will perform the contract.

3. The contract file will contain a record of oral presentations to document what MCCS relied on in making the award decision. The method and level of detail of the record (i.e., MCCS notes, written minutes, videotaping, copies of offeror briefing slides or presentation notes) will be at the discretion of the contracting officer. If the oral presentation includes information that the parties intend to include in the contract, the information will be in writing.

6321. PRICE/FEE ANALYSIS

1. The procurement objective is to promptly satisfy an MCCS requirement at a fair and reasonable price or fee. Determining a fair and reasonable price or fee requires sound judgment by the contracting officer based on pertinent facts. A higher price, or lower fee, compared to other offerors may still be found to be fair and reasonable, and to the best advantage of the MCCS.

2. Price or fee analysis is required with every contract, and will be documented in the Justification for Award memorandum. Adequate competition is the most common basis for determining the proposed price or fee is fair and reasonable.

6322. EVIDENCE OF POSSIBLE COLLUSION BY OFFERORS. If responses to multiple-source solicitations appear to have been arrived at by collusion of the offerors (for example, artificially high or identical prices), the contracting officer will inform MCCS Counsel.

6323. MISTAKES BEFORE AWARD. Contracting officers will review proposals for minor informalities, irregularities and clerical errors. Discussions with offerors to clarify these matters do not constitute negotiation, and usually resolve the inaccuracies. When an award without discussion is considered, the contracting officer will comply with the following:

1. If the contracting officer suspects a mistake, the contracting officer will inform the offeror and request verification. If the offeror verifies the proposal, award may be made;

2. If an offeror alleges a mistake, the contracting officer will advise the offeror that the proposal may be withdrawn, or that correction may be sought as explained in paragraph 3 below;

3. If an offeror requests permission to correct a mistake, the contracting officer may make a written determination permitting the correction, provided that it can be proven that a mistake was made, and provided a legal review is obtained prior to making the determination;

4. If the determination cannot be made and the contracting officer is still considering award without discussion, the offeror will be given final opportunity to withdraw or verify the proposal;

5. If correcting a mistake, however, requires the use of documents, worksheets, or other data outside the solicitation and proposal in order to establish the existence of the mistake, its correction will be considered a matter for negotiation and will open negotiation with other offerors as described in paragraph 6325.

6324. <u>COMPETITIVE RANGE</u>. The contracting officer will determine which proposals are in the competitive range for the purpose of conducting written or oral negotiation. Competitive range is determined by price and other evaluation factors stated in the solicitation and will include all proposals that have a reasonable chance of being selected for award.

6325. <u>CONDUCTING NEGOTIATIONS</u>. Negotiation is a flexible contracting procedure that permits contracting personnel to bargain in the sense of clarification of initial assumptions and positions, give-and-take, and persuasion. These negotiations may apply to price, schedule, technical requirements, or other terms of a proposed contract.

1. The contracting officer may conduct written or oral negotiations with the most competitive offeror, or all offerors in the competitive range (paragraph 6322), without considering the lower technically ranked proposals.

2. The content and extent of the negotiations will be determined by what the contracting officer decides is appropriate.

3. Negotiations will encompass those elements of the solicitation imposing substantial costs on the contractor that may not have been considered or anticipated by the contracting officer when developing the solicitation. If the negotiations fail to achieve a reasonable price, the requiring activity may recommend that the solicitation be canceled.

4. Contracting officers will document the results of negotiations in the Justification for Award memorandum.

6326. <u>JUSTIFICATION FOR AWARD</u>. At the conclusion of evaluation and negotiations, but prior to award, the contracting officer will prepare a Justification for Award memorandum documenting the award decision. All appropriate information regarding the solicitation, solicitation amendments, evaluation findings, any subsequent discussions and negotiations, and the basis for award will be included or referenced in this memorandum. Memorandum content and level of detail is the decision of the contracting officer, but at a minimum, must include a positive determination of contractor responsibility and that the proposed prices or fee are fair and reasonable. Where required, documentation of legal review and award concurrence by a senior MCCS official will be included. The Justification for Award memorandum will be signed by the contracting officer and retained in the contract file.

6327. <u>MAKING THE AWARD</u>. Contracts will be awarded by the contracting officer by signing and dating the contract document and mailing or otherwise furnishing a signed copy of the complete contract to the successful offeror. The contracting officer's signature on the contract affirms that a determination of offeror responsibility and technical acceptability have been made.

1. The contracting officer is responsible for making sure the proposal and/or contract has been signed by an individual having authority to bind the offeror's firm contractually before making the award.

2. Strikeovers, pasteovers, erasures or pen-and-ink changes to the contract document will be avoided, and may only be used for minor changes. If used, such changes will be initialed by the contracting officer and the contractor on the contractor's copy of the contract and the official file copy.

3. The contract becomes effective on the date of award unless a different date is given in the contract itself. Backdating an award date is prohibited.

6328. <u>POST AWARD NOTIFICATION TO OFFERORS</u>. When an award is made using competitive solicitation procedures, the contracting officer will give written notice of award to the successful offeror. When this notice has been issued, the contracting officer will then give written notice to the unsuccessful offerors that their proposals were not accepted. This post award notification will include the name of the successful offeror, and may include the award price. Technical information will not be provided. Upon request of an unsuccessful offeror, the contracting officer will conduct a debrief.

6329. <u>DEBRIEFINGS</u>. A debriefing is an explanation why an offeror did not win a competitive solicitation. During the debrief, the contracting officer should discuss weaknesses in the unsuccessful proposal. However, no unauthorized release of confidential or privileged information may be made during such a discussion. Debriefings will be requested within seven (7) calendar days after notice of contract award. In complex or high dollar procurement actions, the contracting officer will coordinate debrief material with MCCS Counsel prior to the debriefing. The contracting officer will document results of the debriefing and retain in the contract file.

6330. MISTAKES ALLEGED OR DISCOVERED AFTER CONTRACT AWARD

1. When a nonsubstansive mistake is discovered after award, it may be corrected by a modification to the contract, if the correction is favorable to the MCCS and if it does not change the essential requirements of the contract. In all other cases, the contracting officer will review the documentation provided by the contractor and coordinate findings with MCCS Counsel. The contracting officer will consider:

    a. Advice from the requiring activity on whether the item is acceptable to use and will perform its intended task.

    b. A recommendation from the requiring activity (with supporting documentation) on whether to accept or reject the item.

    c. The nature and extent of the contractual adjustment that will result from either decision.

2. If the decision is made to accept the item, the contracting officer will seek an equitable adjustment in the price of the item and negotiate any other adjustments necessary as a result of acceptance. If the decision is made to reject the item, the contracting officer will so notify the contractor and give the contractor the opportunity to correct the problem within the required delivery schedule.

CHAPTER 6

NEGOTIATED PROCUREMENT

SECTION 4: PURCHASE CARD

6400. PURCHASE CARD USE. CMC(MR) will authorize MCCS participation in the Government Commercial Purchase Card program or designate participation in a commercial purchase card program. MCCS activities may not enter into local purchase card programs without prior approval of CMC(MR).

6401. PURCHASE CARD PROGRAM. The Purchase Card program provides a streamlined method of purchasing commercially available supplies and services. The Program Coordinator for MCCS NAF use of the purchase card program is CMC(MR).

1. Agency Program Coordinator. A senior NAF contracting employee should be designated as the MCCS NAF Agency Program Coordinator (APC). The APC will be appointed in writing to manage the purchase card program for the installation MCCS activity. This individual will have overall responsibility for the purchase card program within the MCCS activity. The APC will develop internal purchase card policy, approve who participates in the purchase card program, and issue a delegation of authority to each cardholder who may then obligate NAF funds of the MCCS activity as a purchase cardholder. The APC will suspend or terminate accounts as necessary due to misuse, and report actual or suspected cases of fraud or intent to commit fraud to the MCCS Director and CMC(MR).

2. Delegation of Authority

    a. Cardholders and approving officials will be appointed in writing. Cardholders will be appointed with specific levels of procurement authority identifying their single and monthly purchase limits. Both approving officials and cardholders will complete training and be appointed prior to receiving a NAF purchase card account.

    b. In limited circumstances cardholders may also be appointed as an approving official; however, the cardholder may not be his or her own approving official.

3. Approving Officials. Approving officials will review and sign their cardholders' monthly purchase card statements prior to certifying and forwarding the invoice for payment.

4. Purchase Cardholders. The single purchase limit for cardholders may not exceed $5,000 per order for cardholders, or the warrant authority level for MCCS contracting officers or purchasing agents. All purchases are subject to mandatory sources (UMICOR, NIB/NISH), and purchases in excess of $5,000 must be competed. (Note: The purchase card may not be used to purchase services in excess of $2,500 when the Service Contract Act applies, nor purchase construction in excess of $2,000 when the Davis-Bacon Act applies).

5. Training. All participants (APC, approving officials, and cardholders) will complete required training prior to appointment.

6. _Ethics Standards_. The purchase card is embossed with the cardholder's name and will only be used by that individual. Cardholders in one MCCS branch or activity may not use their card to purchase for another branch or activity unless authorized by the MCCS APC. APCs, approving officials, and cardholders will complete annual ethics training as applicable. Questions will be directed to the local Ethics Counselor or MCCS Counsel.

7. _Prohibited Purchases_. The purchase card will not be used for the following:

    a. Personal Purchases;

    b. Cash Advances;

    c. Rental or lease of land or buildings;

    d. Purchases that require signing of a contract or agreement;

    e. Purchases of official NAF travel related expenses (transportation, lodging, meals, etc).

8. _Regulated Purchases_. Purchase card purchases of the following items are regulated. Refer to your Agency Program Coordinator for specific guidance.

    a. Conference room rentals, A/V equipment, and refreshments;

    b. Merchandise for resale;

    c. Personal clothing or footwear when required by work requirements;

    d. Maintenance and repair services;

    e. Supplies or services to be obtained from designated sources, such as MCCS/installation supply warehouses.

9. _Authorized Purchases_. The purchase card may be used for official purchases at the military exchange and commissary.

10. _Conditions for Use_. Cardholders are authorized to use the purchase card only when the following conditions are met:

    a. Appropriate approvals have been obtained prior to making a purchase;

    b. The supplies and services do not require technical inspection;

    c. Equipment does not require the purchase of extended service warranties or maintenance agreements. These items will be purchased by the MCCS contracting office;

    d. Purchases may not be split into smaller buys to avoid procurement limitations. Requirements exceeding the single purchase limit will be forwarded to the MCCS contracting office;

    e. Purchases are for official U.S. Government/MCCS purposes and are exempt from state and local taxes. Each card is embossed with the words "U.S. Govt. Tax Exempt" for additional clarification.

11. Fixed Asset Exception. Fixed Assets (FA) may not be purchased with the purchase card, unless purchased by a cardholder who is a contacting officer or purchasing agent (see paragraph 2008).

12. Appropriated Fund Purchase Card. MCCS military and civilian personnel may also be designated as appropriated fund purchase cardholders and approving officials. The installation appropriated fund procurement office will provide applicable guidance to these individuals.

MCCS NAF PROCUREMENT POLICY

CHAPTER 7

CONTRACT ADMINISTRATION

SECTION 1: CONTRACT PROTESTS, CLAIMS, DISPUTES AND APPEALS

CHAPTER 7

CONTRACT ADMINISTRATION

7000. <u>GENERAL</u>. Contract administration is the management of a contract from the time of award through its expiration or termination and final retirement of records. The purpose of contract administration is to ensure that the contractor performs according to the contract provisions and that MCCS receives the quantity and quality of the goods or services for which it contracted.

7001. <u>DESIGNATION OF CONTRACTING OFFICER'S REPRESENTATIVE</u>. To aid in the contract administration function, especially where contract performance is remote from the contracting officer's location or program expertise is required, the contracting officer may appoint a Contracting Officer's Representative (COR).

1. COR's are primarily liaisons between the contractor and the contracting officer on technical matters relating to the contract. COR's have no authority other than that which has been delegated to them by the contracting officer.

2. The COR will be selected by the head of the requiring activity, and is usually an individual involved in developing the solicitation specifications, and may have participated in the contract evaluation process.

3. A COR appointment will be made in writing and designated by name and title of position. When it is necessary to change the terms of the appointment, it will be done in an amendment to the appointment or by the issuance of a new appointment. The COR will certify acknowledgement of the appointment letter to indicate an understanding and acceptance of the COR duties and responsibilities.

4. A COR is not delegated authority to make any commitments or changes that affect price, quality, quantity, delivery or other terms and conditions of the contract and may not award a contract or agree to or issue a change to a contract. A contracting officer may authorize a COR to make minor changes, not involving the above items, and to resolve problems as long as such authorizations are not prohibited by the contract. The COR will refer contract interpretation questions to the contracting officer.

5. Upon designating a COR, the contracting officer will provide the COR with a complete copy of the contract, the appointment letter, and any other relevant materials. The contracting officer and COR should jointly develop a contractor surveillance plan to ensure the contractor's performance conforms to contract requirements, is periodically evaluated based on contract criteria, and shortcomings are dealt with expeditiously. The surveillance plan may include such items as timeliness, cleanliness, courtesy to patrons, etc, as required by the contract.

6. COR duties and responsibilities may not be transferred or redelegated to another, unless designated by the contracting officer.

7002. <u>EQUAL EMPLOYMENT OPPORTUNITY AND MINIMUM WAGE NOTICES</u>. The contracting officer will provide Equal Employment Opportunity (EEO) and Minimum Wage notices to the contractor at the time of award.

1. EEO Poster. Every employer covered by the non-discrimination and EEO laws is required to post the "Equal Employment Opportunity is the Law" poster on its premises. The notice must be posted prominently, where it can be readily seen by employees and applicants for employment. The notice provides information concerning the laws and procedures for filing complaints of violations of the laws with the Office of Federal Contract Compliance Programs (OFCCP). [See Executive Order 11246, as amended]. Posters may be obtained from the Internet at: http://www.dol.gov/esa/regs/compliance/posters/eeo.htm

2. Fair Labor Standards Act (FLSA) Minimum Wage Poster. Every employer of employees subject to the Fair Labor Standards Act's minimum wage provisions must post, and keep posted, a notice explaining the Act in a conspicuous place in all of their establishments so as to permit employees to readily read it. The content of the notice is prescribed by the Wage and Hour Division of the Department of Labor. An approved copy of the minimum wage poster is made available for informational purposes or for employers to use as posters at: http://www.dol.gov/esa/regs/compliance/posters/flsa.htm

7003. <u>CONTRACTOR PERFORMANCE FEEDBACK</u>. Contractor nonconformance is usually discovered during quality inspection or as a result of MCCS user or customer complaint. Contractor nonconformance is the failure of a contractor to comply with delivery schedules, performance standards, or other provisions of the contract. The contracting officer must be made aware of the nonconformance, act within the framework of the contract to correct the deficiencies, maintain a suspense file of all deficiencies noted, and follow through with required action until resolved. Documentation of the nonconformance and action taken will be retained in the contract file.

7004. <u>CONTRACT MODIFICATIONS</u>. Contracts may be modified using appropriate forms and procedures. All contract modifications begin at number one (1) regardless of any solicitation amendments. Modifications to contracts are either unilateral (signed by only the contracting officer) or bilateral (signed by both the contractor and contracting officer) actions. All modifications will be documented in a memorandum explaining the action. The memorandum will be signed by the contracting officer and retained in the contract file.

7005. <u>OPTION CLAUSES</u>

1. An option clause may allow MCCS to purchase additional supplies or services or to extend the period of the contract, if the action is taken within the time specified in the contract's option clause, and when determined to be in the best interest of the MCCS. Option clauses will not be used when:

    a. The supplies or services are readily available on the open market at better prices;

    b. The contractor will incur undue risk, such as the inability to estimate the price or availability of required materials and labor for future requirements;

    c. Market prices for supplies or services are likely to change substantially.

2. Prior to exercising an option clause, the contracting officer and COR will review the quality and timeliness of the supplies or services provided. The results of this review will be documented and retained in the contract file.

7006. <u>CHANGE ORDERS</u>. The Changes clause of the contract permits the contracting officer to make unilateral changes in those areas identified in the clause, and provides an equitable adjustment to the contractor if the change causes an increase or decrease in the cost of the work or in the time required for performance. Change orders can place undue hardships on contractors, and should not be used if a mutually agreeable modification can be negotiated, which is the preferred method.

7007. <u>CONSTRUCTIVE CHANGES</u>. Constructive changes are defined as any conduct by a contracting officer or other authorized representative, other than a formal change order or supplemental agreement, which has the effect of requiring the contractor to perform new work or different work from that required by the contract. Such changes entitle the contractor to relief under the Changes clause and will be avoided.

7008. <u>NOVATION AGREEMENT</u>. A Novation Agreement is used to transfer the operation or performance of a contract to another party. In the novation, the NAF contracting officer agrees to recognize the third party as a successor in interest to the MCCS contract. Novations may be approved where it would provide advantages such as continued performance of the contract. Novations should not be used where it appears the contractor's motive is to sell the contract soon after award or otherwise gain a profit from a "buy in."

1. A novation agreement is not used to change the name of a contractor when no change in ownership occurs. A contract modification is used for this purpose.

2. Under a novation agreement, the new party (transferee), with MCCS consent, takes over from the contractor (transferor) and assumes responsibility for performance of the contract and provides certificates of insurance as required. Based on the terms of the novation, the former contractor may be relieved of all future responsibility for prior actions under the contract.

3. MCCS may recognize a third party as a successor in interest to an MCCS contract under any of these circumstances:

    a. The third party's interest is incidental to the transfer of all assets of the contractor;

    b. The third party's interest is incidental to the transfer of that part of the contractor's assets involved in the performance of the contract;

    c. The contractor requests to transfer interest in a contract to a successor for continued performance. Examples of such circumstances include, but are not limited to, sale of assets by a contractor, transfer of such under a merger or consolidation, and incorporation of a proprietorship or partnership;

    d. Novating the contract is more advantageous to MCCS than terminating the contract and resoliciting or allowing the contract to expire.

4. When a contractor requests MCCS recognize a successor in interest, the contractor will be required to furnish the contracting officer with documentary evidence that the successor in interest is a responsible contractor, such as:

    a. Evidence of experience, financial and technical ability, or other capability of the transferee to perform the contract;

    b. Written consent of the sureties on contracts where bonds are required;

    c. In the case of patron or retail service contracts involving processing customer owned property or customer orders, an inventory of unclaimed customer orders or orders in progress, acknowledged by the transferee.

5. When the novation is due to a contractor transferring or selling its assets, the contractor will be required to provide evidence of the sale, such as a bill of sale, certificate of merger, resolution of the board of directors, or copy of the certificate and articles of incorporation.

6. When the decision has been made to recognize a successor in interest to an MCCS contract, the contracting officer will execute a novation agreement with the transferee and transferor. This three-way contract modification will be assigned a consecutive contract modification number. The contracting officer will complete a Memorandum for the Record to document the action. A novation format is available from CMC(MR).

7. A contract in which a novation has been executed will be considered to have been in force from the effective date of the original contract.

7009. DELAYS IN DELIVERY OR PERFORMANCE

1. Excusable delays are due to causes beyond the control of the contractor. The standard procedure to be used in the case of an excusable delay is to extend the delivery or performance schedule by a bilateral modification to the contract. If the goods or performance are required before the contractor can deliver, the contract may be terminated for convenience.

2. Inexcusable delays are not due to causes beyond the control of the contractor. A thorough analysis of the situation and possible courses of action should be made to determine the most efficient and economical method of resolution. MCCS Counsel will be consulted for any situation involving an inexcusable delay.

7010. FINANCIAL OBLIGATIONS. All MCCS financial obligations will be processed in a timely manner as called for by the Prompt Payment Act (31 U.S.C. Section 3901 et. seq.). Failure to meet contract payment obligations will result in the requirement for MCCS to pay interest to the contractor. Failure to make interest payments on time may result in the accrual of additional penalties for MCCS.

7011. MODIFICATION EFFECTIVE DATES. Unless indicated otherwise, the effective date of a contract modification is the date it is signed by the contracting officer.

CHAPTER 7

CONTRACT ADMINISTRATION

SECTION 1: CONTRACT PROTESTS, CLAIMS, DISPUTES AND APPEALS

7100. <u>RELEASING INFORMATION</u>. In all instances of protests, claims, disputes or appeals regarding a procurement action, there will be no release of information regarding the procurement when a simple explanation (such as name of the awardee or contract price) will resolve the inquiry. If detailed information or procurement documents are sought, the approval of MCCS Counsel will be obtained prior to release.

7101. <u>PROTESTS</u>. The first step in resolving any concern or issue raised by an offeror is for the contracting officer to consider the matter and respond to the offeror accordingly. Many times, a concern or issue raised by an offeror may be resolved with a simple explanation of the reason for the contracting officer's decision. Where the concern or issue cannot be resolved through informal discussion between the contracting officer and offeror, the offeror must file a written protest for the matter to be considered further.

1. Only interested parties may file protests. An interested party is an actual or prospective offeror whose direct economic interest would be affected by the award or failure to award a particular contract.

2. The contracting officer is responsible for promptly processing or resolving all protests received. Protests may be received either before or after contract award. Any protest lodged with other than the contracting activity will be referred or sent immediately to the appropriate contracting officer.

3. Upon receipt of a protest, the contracting officer will notify MCCS Counsel.

4. Protests that cannot be resolved by meeting with the protester or that the contracting officer determines have no merit, require a written decision and reply to the protester by the contracting officer explaining the rationale for the decision.

5. The contracting officer will document the results of all protest actions, including advise of Counsel, in a memorandum and retain in the solicitation or contract file.

7102. <u>PROTESTS BEFORE AWARD</u>

1. Protests based on alleged improprieties in a solicitation that are apparent on the face of the solicitation must be filed with the contracting officer, in writing, before the closing date for receipt of proposals. Protests to the contents of an amendment to the solicitation must be filed, in writing, before the closing date (or amended closing date) for receipt of proposals of the amendment.

2. When a protest is received before contract award, the award will be delayed until the protest (including appeals) is resolved, unless the contracting officer determines that one of the following applies:

    a. The supplies or services are urgently required;

    b. Delivery or performance will be unduly delayed by failure to make a prompt award;

    c. The current contract is expiring and continued service is required;

    d. A timely award will otherwise be advantageous to the MCCS.

3. Before awarding a contract under the above-cited circumstances, the advice of MCCS Counsel will be obtained. The Justification for Award memorandum will fully document the award decision and be retained in the contract file.

4. If the contracting officer delays award of the contract, he or she will conduct discussions or convene whatever meetings or conferences are necessary to determine the merits of the protest. When the contracting officer finds a protest has merit (e.g., ambiguous specifications, flawed evaluation process), he or she will promptly take action to correct the situation. Such possible actions include, rejecting all proposals and issuing a new or amended solicitation, revising specifications, or changing evaluation criteria. In amended solicitations, the receipt date of proposals will be extended accordingly. If resolution of the protest makes previously ineligible offerors eligible for award, appropriate notification will be given to the offerors concerned.

7103. <u>PROTESTS AFTER AWARD</u>

1. All protests will be handled expeditiously. The contracting officer will give a copy of the protest to the awardee, to any interested party, and to appropriate MCCS personnel. The contracting officer may allow any party so notified to submit written comments regarding the protest for consideration by the contracting officer. The time limit for such comments to be filed should be established by the contracting officer when the party is notified of the protest. Where the protest contains information claimed by the protester to be procurement sensitive or otherwise protected from disclosure, the contracting officer should send a summary of the grounds of protest and not an actual copy of the protest, unless the protester or contracting officer has redacted the protected information (Refer to paragraph 7104). MCCS personnel in procurement and requirements positions may not disclose protected information or procurement sensitive information.

2. A protest will be lodged in writing within ten (10) days of notification of contract award to be considered. When a protest is received by the contracting officer after the contract has been awarded, contract performance need not be suspended or terminated, unless it appears likely the award may be invalidated and non-delivery or non-performance is not prejudicial to the activity's interest. If the protester presents compelling reasons why contract performance is to be postponed or suspended, the contracting officer will promptly notify the awardee, in writing, and will provide instructions regarding the postponement or suspension of contract performance. If the protester presents compelling reasons why the award should be invalidated, the contracting officer will attempt to negotiate a mutual agreement with the awardee for performance to be suspended at no-cost, until the protest is resolved. If a no cost suspension cannot be negotiated, seek the advice of MCCS Counsel.

7104. CLAIMS OF PROCUREMENT SENSITIVE INFORMATION. The burden to show that information is procurement sensitive or otherwise protected from disclosure is on the party making the claim for withholding. Where the protest or comments filed by an interested party contain information clearly marked as being procurement sensitive or otherwise protected from disclosure, the contracting officer should take steps to safeguard the information pending further investigation into the matter. For example, when notifying a party of a protest, the contracting officer should delete or redact any such information before sending a copy of the protest. The contracting officer will coordinate offeror claims of procurement sensitive information with MCCS Counsel prior to action.

7105. APPEALS OF THE CONTRACTING OFFICER'S PROTEST DECISION

1. Protests that cannot be resolved at a conference or that the contracting officer determines have no merit require a written decision by the contracting officer to the protester explaining the rationale for the decision. The contracting officer's decision must inform how it may be appealed. The protester's appeal should reference the contracting officer's decision and explain that an appeal is intended. The notice to the protester will include the following: "You are advised that you may appeal this decision within ten (10) calendar days from receipt of this letter by mailing or otherwise furnishing a written appeal addressed to (insert the full mailing address of the Installation Commander). The Installation Commander's protest decision is final and may not be further appealed."

2. Only matters raised in the original protest may be appealed. An offeror may not raise new issues or grounds for protest not considered by the contracting officer. Appeals raising new issues or grounds for protest will be dismissed by the appeal authority.

3. Upon notification of a protest appeal the contracting officer will forward a completely documented solicitation or contract file to MCCS Counsel to include:

    a. The letter or document that initiated the protest, together with all supporting evidence submitted by the person making the protest;

    b. A copy of the proposal of the protesting offeror and a copy of the proposal of the offeror who is being considered for award, or the successful proposal;

    c. Any other documents relevant to the protest;

    d. A copy of the contracting officer's protest decision; and

    e. A statement signed by the contracting officer setting forth a preliminary analysis of the matter, together with any additional information or evidence considered necessary in determining the validity of the protest.

4. The Installation Commander or designee will obtain the written advice of MCCS Counsel before deciding the appeal. The standard of review for the decision on the protest appeal is whether the contracting officer's denial of the protest was arbitrary, capricious, an abuse of discretion, or a violation of applicable law or regulation. The installation commander must respond to the appeal in writing within thirty days of receipt.

7106. <u>INVALIDATED AWARD</u>. If a contract award is to be terminated as a result of the protest decision, or protest appeal decision, the contracting officer will seek a mutual agreement with the awardee to stop performance on a no-cost basis. Should this not be possible, a termination for convenience will be initiated.

7107. <u>CONTRACT CLAIMS</u>

1. Whenever a contractor requests a change in the terms of the contract, whether monetary or otherwise, the contracting officer will determine whether it is a claim or merely a routine request for contract modification. A claim is defined as a written demand or written assertion by one of the contracting parties seeking, as a matter of right, the payment of a specific amount of money ("a sum certain"), the adjustment or interpretation of contract terms, or other relief arising under or relating to the contract. Contractor claims must be submitted to the contracting officer per the Disputes Clause contained in the contract. Upon receipt of a claim, the contracting officer will immediately forward a copy of the claim to MCCS Counsel.

2. MCCS may also submit claims against the contractor. Prior to submitting any such claim, the contracting officer will coordinate with MCCS Counsel.

7108. <u>DISPUTES</u>

1. Disputes are a disagreement between the contractor and the contracting officer regarding the rights and obligations of the parties under a contract. It is the duty of the contracting officer to make every reasonable attempt to resolve the dispute amicably without resort to the Disputes clause. Due to the unique nature of the MCCS, two different versions of the Disputes clause are used. The contracting officer will ensure the correct contract Disputes clause is included in the solicitation and resulting contract:

    a. Marine Corps Exchange (MCX). Contracts for the purchase of resale merchandise, equipment, supplies, services, and revenue generating activities for the MCX will reference the Contract Disputes Act (41 U.S.C. Sec. 602 et. seq.).

    b. Marine Corps Morale, Welfare and Recreation (MWR). Contracts for the purchase of equipment, supplies, services, and MWR revenue generating activities will not reference the Contract Disputes Act (28 U.S.C. Sec. 1346 and Sec. 1491) or the Armed Services Board of Contract Appeals.

2. Contact MCCS Counsel for additional guidance.

7109. <u>DISPUTE PROCEDURE</u>

1. If attempts to resolve the dispute fail, the contracting officer will first request the contractor to state the facts of the dispute in writing. The contracting officer will review all available facts pertinent to the dispute, and obtain the assistance of legal, technical, and professional experts. The contracting officer will render a final decision after an independent review of all the facts.

2. The contracting officer's decision must be in writing. It will include a statement of all facts sufficient to enable the contractor to understand both the decision and the basis for the determination. Normally, the decision will be in the form of a statement of the claim or other description of the nature of the dispute, with necessary references to pertinent contract provisions. It will include a statement of the relevant facts to which the parties agree and, as clearly as possible, the area of disagreement. The contracting officer's statement will include his or her decision, and advise the contractor on the process to appeal the decision.

3. The contracting officer's decision will be mailed to the contractor by certified mail, return receipt requested. Dispute decisions will be reviewed by MCCS Counsel prior to release to the contractor.

7110. APPEALS OF THE CONTRACTING OFFICER'S DISPUTE DECISION. Under the Disputes clause in the contract, the contractor may appeal the decision of the contracting officer.

1. The appeal process for Exchange contracts is governed by the Contract Disputes Act (CDA). Under the CDA, the contractor may appeal the contracting officer's decision by mailing or otherwise furnishing to the contracting officer a written appeal addressed to the Armed Services Board of Contract Appeals (ASBCA) within 90 days, or filing an action in the United States Court of Federal Claims within 12 months, of receipt of the contracting officer's decision.

2. The appeal process for MWR contracts requires the contractor to appeal the contracting officer's dispute decision by mailing or otherwise furnishing the written appeal to the Installation Commander and furnishing a copy of the appeal to the contracting officer within 90 days of receipt of the contracting officer's decision. The Installation Commander's decision, which should be made expeditiously, is final and not appealable.

3. If coordinated with MCCS Counsel prior to contract award, an Alternate Dispute Resolution (ADR) clause may be included in the contract.

4. The decision reached in the appeal (or ADR) process is final.

5. Pending final decision on an appeal in any dispute, the contracting officer will advise the contractor of his duty to proceed with contract performance and in accordance with the contracting officer's decision.

6. The contracting officer will document the result of all disputes and appeals, including the advice of Counsel and the basis for the contracting officer's decision, in a memorandum and retain in the contract file.

CHAPTER 7

CONTRACT ADMINISTRATION

SECTION 2: CONTRACT TERMINATION

7200. <u>TERMINATION OF CONTRACTS</u>

1. Generally, MCCS contract clauses provide that contracts may be terminated for contractor default, MCCS convenience, or inactivation of installation or MCCS activity; or

2. If included in the contract, MCCS contracts may also be terminated by written notice by either party to the other party within a designated period of time or by mutual consent of both parties. Refer to paragraph 7209.

3. Since termination of a contract may cause a lapse of service, a shortage of supply, or require a quick response by other MCCS offices, the contracting officer will notify appropriate offices of pending termination actions.

7201. <u>CONTRACTOR DEFAULT</u>. A contracting officer's major objective is to ensure that MCCS receives the goods or services required in the quality, quantity and at the time and place required. If a contractor does not comply with contract terms, it may be appropriate to terminate the contract for default. A contract may be terminated for default only after coordination with MCCS Counsel.

7202. <u>CORRECTIVE ACTIONS PRIOR TO TERMINATION FOR DEFAULT</u>. Minor operational deficiencies not amounting to a breach of contract which exist because of the contractor's failure to comply with contractual requirements, but do not seriously affect MCCS operations or patron service, should normally be resolved by oral requests to the contractor by the contracting officer or the MCCS representative responsible for the contract surveillance. At the option of the contracting officer, a warning letter may be issued.

7203. <u>CURE LETTERS</u>. When a contractor fails to comply with oral requests or warning letters and the frequency of noncompliance or the magnitude of contract deficiencies warrants additional action, the contracting officer will issue a cure letter.

1. A cure letter formally advises a contractor of specific failures to comply with the contract and requires corrective action within a specified time. If the contractor fails to cure the performance, normally the contracting officer will initiate termination action by issuing a show-cause letter.

2. Cure letters will reference the contract number, contract date, and describe the acts or omissions constituting the default and cite the contract clauses that have been breached.

3. Cure letters will not be issued to contractors when MCCS is participating in or issuing delivery orders against other NAF or appropriated fund contracts. The

issuing NAF or appropriated fund contracting officer that issued the contract is the official responsible for issuing a cure letter in such an instance.

7204. SHOW-CAUSE AND FORBEARANCE LETTERS

1. If a contractor fails to cure performance, the contracting officer should issue a show-cause or forbearance letter. The show-cause and forbearance letters advise the contractor of the contracting officer's intent to terminate the contract for default unless the failure was due to causes beyond the control and without the fault or negligence of the contractor. Fires, flood, epidemics, quarantine restrictions, freight embargoes, strikes, and other events that preclude performance through no fault of the contractor are normally excusable reasons for nonperformance.

2. Show-cause and forbearance letters will reference the contract number, contract date, and describe the acts or omissions constituting the default and cite the contract clauses that have been breached. The show-cause and forbearance letters will require the contractor to respond in writing to the circumstances that caused the breach of contract.

3. For service contracts, if the contractor fails to cure the default within the period specified in the cure letter, the contracting officer may issue a letter of forbearance instead of a show-cause letter. The letter of forbearance will advise the contractor that if the contractor defaults again within the time specified (usually three months), the contracting officer will immediately issue a default termination at that time.

4. The contracting officer will seek guidance from MCCS Counsel prior to issuing show-cause or forbearance letters.

7205. TERMINATION FOR DEFAULT. When termination for default is appropriate, the contracting officer normally will issue a Notice of Termination for Default. The termination notice will:

1. Include the contract number and contract award date.

2. Describe the acts or omissions constituting the default and cite the contract clauses that have been breached.

3. Cite the fact there has either been no reply to the cure letter, show-cause letter or forbearance letter, or that the contractor has failed to show the default was beyond their control and without fault or negligence.

4. Establish a definite termination date.

5. The contracting officer will obtain from the MCCS accounting office the amount of any debts due MCCS and coordinate with Counsel and other contracting officers regarding collection of this debt from the contractor's operation(s) at other MCCS activities.

6. Other factors to consider include the previous payment of any advance or progress payments, costs on undelivered work, profit on uncompleted items, and reprocurement costs.

7. In revenue-generating patron service or vending contracts, the contracting officer will coordinate with Counsel regarding exercising MCCS's contractual right to take possession of the contractor's equipment on the installation to satisfy these debts.

7206. <u>LEGAL REVIEW AND PROCESSING</u>. The contracting officer will coordinate cure, show-cause, forbearance and termination actions, and withdrawal of termination letters, with MCCS Counsel. On coordination with Counsel, cure and show-cause letters may be dispensed with, or a combination of cure and show-cause letters may be issued.

7207. <u>TERMINATION FOR CONVENIENCE</u>

1. Terminations for convenience are normally used when the MCCS no longer has a need for the supplies or services under contract. The termination for convenience provides for an equitable adjustment to the contractor for work already performed. It does not entitle a subcontractor to a claim against the MCCS.

2. In the event a contract must be terminated for convenience of the MCCS, the contracting officer will attempt to terminate the contract on a no-cost basis to either party. If this is not possible, the contractor will be required to submit a claim to the contracting officer in writing. A settlement should compensate the contractor fairly for the work done and the preparations made for the terminated portion of the contract, if any, and profit on completed work. If an equitable adjustment cannot be negotiated, the contracting officer will make a final decision concerning the claim, in writing, and provide this to the contractor in a timely manner. Any dispute arising as a result of this process will be resolved using the Disputes process.

3. As a general rule, a Termination for Convenience may not be used to terminate a defaulting contractor, nor be immediately followed by a new contract for the same requirement.

7208. <u>TERMINATION BASED ON INACTIVATION</u>. When a contract is terminated based on inactivation of an installation or MCCS activity, normally the contracting officer will advise the contractor in writing at the earliest possible date of termination. The letter will cite the clause that provides for termination of the contract because of inactivation of the installation or MCCS activity and the date of termination.

7209. <u>ALTERNATE TERMINATION METHODS</u>

1. Mutual Termination. Contracts may be terminated by mutual consent via a bilateral modification to the contract.

2. Notice termination. A contract may be terminated by MCCS or the contractor by written notice to the other party within the specified notice period, provided this termination clause is included in the contract. The specified time period is normally 30 to 90 days, so that the MCCS may have time to negotiate a new contract.

a. Upon receipt of a notice termination, the contracting officer will acknowledge the notice in writing, clearly establish the time and date of termination, and direct other action as appropriate.

b. If notice is not provided in writing or within the specified time period, and the contractor pursues termination, the contract may be in default.

7210. <u>CONTRACTOR CLAIMS IN CONJUNCTION WITH TERMINATION</u>. Termination of a contract is not in itself a final decision on a contractor claim. If, after a termination notice is received, a contractor requests monetary or other relief, the contracting officer will coordinate appropriate action with MCCS Counsel.

7211. <u>RELEASE OF CLAIMS</u>. MCCS will obtain a Release of Claims, which absolves the MCCS from further contractor claims, as part of all termination actions. Consult MCCS Counsel for additional guidance.

7212. <u>CONTRACT CLOSEOUT</u>. Contracts are considered to be closed when:

1. The contractor has completed the required deliveries and the equipment or supplies have been accepted by the MCCS; and

2. The contractor has performed all services and they have been accepted by the MCCS; and

3. All option provisions have expired, or MCCS elects not to exercise option provisions; and

4. Final payment has been made.

7213. <u>ELECTRONIC SYSTEM CLOSEOUT</u>. Completed procurement actions in the electronic procurement system will be closed-out and cancelled so the records are purged from the system. Most purchase orders and delivery orders will be closed annually. Multi-year contracts may remain open until contract completion.

7214. <u>RETIRING CONTRACT FILES</u>

1. When a contract expires through termination or otherwise, the file will be retired through procedures set out in SECNAVINST 5212.5D, Records Disposition Manual. Identify contracts by number on the outside of storage boxes, and in a file retained in the procurement office, so contracts may be easily retrieved should the need arise.

2. If a claim or dispute is involved, the contract file will not be retired until the claim or dispute is settled.

www.ingramcontent.com/pod-product-compliance
Lightning Source LLC
Chambersburg PA
CBHW081108290526
45795CB00006B/2042